Instagram Marketing for Business

A Step-by-Step Guide to Growing Your Audience and Building a Successful Brand on Instagram

Heinrich Brevis

Table of Contents

Introduction

Welcome to "Instagram Marketing for Business: A Step-by-Step Guide to Growing Your Audience and Building a Successful Brand on Instagram." Whether you are a seasoned marketer or just starting, this guide is designed to help you harness the full potential of Instagram to grow your audience and build a thriving brand.

The Power of Instagram

Instagram has transformed from a simple photo-sharing app into one of the most powerful marketing tools available today. With over a billion active users, it offers an unparalleled platform for businesses to connect with their audience, showcase their products, and build a strong brand presence. The visual nature of Instagram makes it an ideal medium for storytelling, engaging content, and direct interaction with your target audience.

Why Instagram Marketing Matters

In today's digital age, traditional marketing methods alone are no longer sufficient. Consumers are looking for authenticity, visual appeal, and real-time engagement, all of which Instagram excels at providing. An effective Instagram marketing strategy can help you:

- **Increase Brand Awareness**: Reach a wider audience and make your brand recognizable.

- **Boost Engagement**: Interact with your customers in a meaningful way, fostering loyalty and trust.
- **Drive Traffic and Sales**: Use Instagram's features to guide followers to your website or e-commerce platform, converting them into customers.
- **Build Community**: Create a community of loyal followers who advocate for your brand.

What You Will Learn

This book is structured to take you through every aspect of Instagram marketing, from setting up your business profile to advanced strategies for growth and engagement. Here's a glimpse of what each chapter covers:

- **Chapter 1**: An introduction to the fundamentals of Instagram marketing, including the platform's algorithm and key metrics.
- **Chapter 2**: A guide to setting up and optimizing your business profile to make a strong first impression.
- **Chapter 3**: Strategies for developing a content plan that balances various types of posts and keeps your audience engaged.
- **Chapter 4**: Techniques for growing your audience organically and through partnerships.
- **Chapter 5**: Insights into creating effective Instagram ads and measuring their performance.
- **Chapter 6**: Methods for engaging with your followers and retaining their interest.
- **Chapter 7**: Advanced strategies for leveraging Instagram's features to enhance your brand presence.
- **Chapter 8**: Tools and tips for analyzing your performance and adapting your strategy to stay ahead of the competition.

Who This Book Is For

This book is designed for entrepreneurs, small business owners, marketers, and anyone looking to enhance their brand's presence on Instagram. Whether you're aiming to increase your followers, boost engagement, or drive sales, you'll find practical advice and actionable strategies tailored to your needs.

How to Use This Book

You can read this book cover to cover to get a comprehensive understanding of Instagram marketing, or you can skip to the chapters that are most relevant to your current needs. Each chapter includes step-by-step instructions, tips, and real-world examples to help you apply what you learn immediately.

The Journey Ahead

Instagram marketing is an ever-evolving field, with new features and trends emerging regularly. This guide aims to equip you with the foundational knowledge and skills to navigate this dynamic landscape successfully. As you implement these strategies, you'll not only grow your audience but also build a brand that resonates with your followers and stands out in the crowded digital marketplace.

Chapter 1: Introduction to Instagram Marketing

In the bustling, ever-evolving landscape of social media, one platform has emerged as a beacon for marketers worldwide: Instagram. With over a billion active users and a unique blend of visual storytelling and community engagement, Instagram offers an unparalleled opportunity to connect with audiences meaningfully. Whether you're a small business owner, an aspiring influencer, or a seasoned marketer, understanding the nuances of Instagram marketing is essential to harnessing its full potential.

The Rise of Instagram

Instagram's journey from a simple photo-sharing app to a global marketing powerhouse is remarkable. Launched in 2010 by Kevin Systrom and Mike Krieger, Instagram quickly captivated users with its intuitive interface and the ability to transform mundane moments into visually appealing snapshots. The app's growth was meteoric, reaching one million users in just two months and 10 million within a year.

Facebook's acquisition of Instagram in 2012 for $1 billion was a pivotal moment, not only in the platform's history but also in the broader context of social media marketing. This acquisition fueled Instagram's expansion, introducing new features like video sharing, direct messaging, and, most importantly for marketers, advertising capabilities.

Why Instagram Matters for Marketers

Instagram's appeal lies in its highly engaged user base and the visual-centric nature of its content. Unlike other social platforms where text dominates, Instagram is all about visuals—photos, videos, and now, Stories and Reels. This visual focus makes it an ideal platform for brands looking to showcase their products and services creatively and authentically.

High Engagement Rates

One of the most compelling reasons to invest in Instagram marketing is the platform's high engagement rates. Studies consistently show that Instagram users interact with content more frequently than users on other social networks. This means your posts, stories, and ads are more likely to be seen, liked, and shared, driving greater brand awareness and loyalty.

Targeted Advertising

Instagram's advertising platform, integrated with Facebook's powerful ad manager, allows for precise targeting. You can reach your ideal audience based on demographics, interests, behaviors, and even purchase history. This level of targeting ensures that your marketing efforts are not only reaching a broad audience but the right audience.

Community Building

Beyond advertising, Instagram is a powerful tool for community building. Brands can foster a sense of belonging and loyalty by engaging with their audience through comments, direct messages, and interactive content like polls and questions in Stories. This two-way interaction is invaluable in building trust and long-term relationships with your customers.

Understanding Instagram's Core Features

To effectively market on Instagram, it's crucial to understand its core features and how to leverage them. Let's delve into the primary components of the platform.

The Feed

The Instagram feed is the heart of the platform, where users scroll through a curated stream of photos and videos from accounts they follow. For marketers, the feed is a prime real estate for showcasing high-quality, visually appealing content that resonates with your audience. Consistency in posting and maintaining a cohesive aesthetic can significantly enhance your brand's presence.

Stories

Instagram Stories, introduced in 2016, are ephemeral posts that disappear after 24 hours. Stories offer a more casual and spontaneous way to connect with your audience. They can include photos, videos, text, and interactive elements like polls and quizzes. For marketers, Stories are a versatile tool for sharing behind-the-scenes content, promotions, and engaging directly with followers in real time.

Reels

Reels, Instagram's answer to TikTok, allow users to create short, engaging videos set to music. Reels are designed for discoverability, appearing in a dedicated section and often featured prominently on the Explore page. This makes Reels an excellent opportunity for reaching new audiences and going viral with creative, entertaining content.

IGTV

IGTV is Instagram's long-form video platform, supporting videos up to an hour in length. It's ideal for more in-depth content like tutorials, interviews, and product demos. IGTV videos can be previewed in your feed, driving viewers to watch the full video on IGTV.

Shopping

Instagram Shopping transforms the platform into a seamless e-commerce experience. Businesses can tag products in their posts and Stories, allowing users to purchase directly from the app. This feature is a game-changer for brands, turning engagement into sales with minimal friction.

Crafting Your Instagram Marketing Strategy

Developing a successful Instagram marketing strategy involves a combination of creativity, analytics, and a deep understanding of your audience. Here are some key steps to get started:

Define Your Goals

What do you want to achieve with Instagram marketing? Whether it's increasing brand awareness, driving website traffic, generating leads, or boosting sales, having clear, measurable goals is the first step in crafting a strategy.

Know Your Audience

Understanding your target audience is critical. Use Instagram Insights and other analytics tools to gather data on your followers' demographics, interests, and behaviors. This information will guide your content creation and advertising efforts.

Create Compelling Content

Content is king on Instagram. Invest in high-quality visuals and experiment with different formats like photos, videos, Stories, and Reels. Keep your content diverse but consistent with your brand's voice and aesthetic.

Engage with Your Community

Building a community requires active engagement. Respond to comments, answer direct messages, and participate in conversations. Use interactive features like polls, questions, and live videos to foster a sense of connection.

Analyze and Adapt

Regularly review your performance metrics to understand what's working and what's not. Use this data to refine your strategy, experiment with new content types, and stay ahead of trends.

The Future of Instagram Marketing

As Instagram continues to evolve, so do the opportunities for marketers. Emerging technologies like augmented reality (AR) and artificial intelligence (AI) are set to transform the way we create and consume content on the platform. Instagram's focus on shopping and e-commerce will likely expand, offering even more integrated purchasing experiences.

In this dynamic environment, staying informed and adaptable is key. By leveraging Instagram's unique features and understanding its audience, you can craft compelling campaigns that resonate, engage, and drive results.

Welcome to the world of Instagram marketing—a vibrant, ever-changing landscape where creativity and strategy intersect to create endless possibilities. As you embark on this journey, remember that success on Instagram is not just about gaining followers but building genuine connections and delivering value to your audience.

1.1 Setting Clear Marketing Goals and Objectives

The foundation of any successful marketing campaign, whether on Instagram or any other platform, lies in setting clear, actionable goals and objectives. Without defined targets, your efforts can become disjointed, making it difficult to measure success or adjust strategies effectively. This section will guide you through the process of establishing robust marketing goals and objectives tailored to Instagram's unique environment.

Understanding the Importance of Goals and Objectives

Goals and objectives serve as your roadmap, providing direction and purpose to your marketing activities. They help you stay focused, allocate resources efficiently, and measure your progress. For Instagram marketing, these goals might range from increasing brand visibility to driving sales or enhancing customer engagement.

Differentiating Goals and Objectives

It's essential to distinguish between goals and objectives:

- **Goals**: These are broad, overarching aspirations that describe what you want to achieve. They are long-term and often qualitative.
- **Objectives**: These are specific, measurable actions that support your goals. They are short to medium-term and quantitative, providing clear metrics for success.

For example, a goal might be to "enhance brand awareness," while an objective could be to "increase Instagram followers by 20% in the next six months."

Setting SMART Goals

One of the most effective frameworks for setting goals and objectives is the SMART criteria. SMART stands for Specific, Measurable, Achievable, Relevant, and Time-bound. Let's break down each component:

- **Specific**: Goals should be unambiguous. Instead of saying, "I want more followers," specify, "I want to gain 1,000 new followers."
- **Measurable**: There should be a way to track progress. Use metrics like follower count, engagement rates, and website traffic to measure success.
- **Achievable**: Goals should be realistic given your resources and current situation. Ambitious goals are good, but they should still be attainable.
- **Relevant**: Ensure your goals align with your broader business objectives and are relevant to your target audience.
- **Time-bound**: Set a deadline for achieving your goals. This creates a sense of urgency and helps maintain focus.

Common Instagram Marketing Goals

To help you get started, here are some common Instagram marketing goals and examples of corresponding SMART objectives:

Increase Brand Awareness

- Objective: "Grow our Instagram followers by 30% over the next six months."
- Objective: "Achieve an average of 500 likes per post within three months."

Boost Engagement

- Objective: "Increase our average engagement rate from 2% to 4% in the next quarter."
- Objective: "Double the number of comments on our posts by the end of the year."

Drive Website Traffic

- Objective: "Generate 1,000 website visits per month from Instagram by the end of Q3."
- Objective: "Achieve a 5% click-through rate on Instagram Stories with swipe-up links in the next two months."

Generate Leads

- Objective: "Collect 500 new email subscribers through Instagram lead generation campaigns within the next three months."

- Objective: "Achieve a 10% conversion rate on Instagram ads targeting our new product launch."

Increase Sales

- Objective: "Drive $10,000 in sales directly from Instagram Shopping within the next quarter."
- Objective: "Achieve a 20% increase in product page visits from Instagram ads by the end of the year."

Aligning Goals with Your Business Strategy

Your Instagram marketing goals should align seamlessly with your overall business strategy. This alignment ensures that your efforts on Instagram contribute directly to your broader objectives, whether they are related to sales growth, market expansion, or brand positioning.

For instance, if your business strategy focuses on entering new markets, your Instagram goals might include targeting followers in specific geographic regions or collaborating with local influencers. If product innovation is a priority, your goals might involve showcasing new products through Instagram Reels or IGTV videos.

Regularly Reviewing and Adjusting Goals

The digital landscape, including Instagram, is constantly evolving. What worked six months ago might not be as effective today. Regularly reviewing and adjusting your goals and objectives is crucial for staying relevant and maximizing your efforts.

Set aside time quarterly to assess your progress. Analyze your performance metrics, identify trends, and adjust your goals as needed. This iterative process ensures that your Instagram marketing strategy remains dynamic and responsive to changes in the market and your business environment.

Setting clear marketing goals and objectives is the cornerstone of a successful Instagram marketing strategy. By defining what you want to achieve and establishing specific, measurable, achievable, relevant, and time-bound objectives, you create a roadmap that guides your efforts and maximizes your impact. Remember, the key to effective goal-setting is alignment with your broader business strategy and a commitment to regular review and adjustment. With clear goals in place, you're well on your way to leveraging Instagram's powerful platform to achieve remarkable results.

1.2 Key Metrics to Track for Success

To ensure the effectiveness of your Instagram marketing strategy, it's essential to monitor key performance indicators (KPIs) that provide insight into your progress and success. By tracking these metrics, you can make informed decisions, refine your strategy, and ultimately achieve your marketing goals. This section will explore the critical metrics you should monitor to gauge the success of your Instagram marketing efforts.

Engagement Metrics

Engagement metrics measure how your audience interacts with your content. High engagement indicates that your content resonates with your audience, fostering a deeper connection with your brand.

- **Likes**: The number of likes on your posts is a basic but important measure of popularity and user appreciation.
- **Comments**: Comments provide a deeper level of engagement, reflecting your audience's willingness to interact and share their thoughts. Monitoring the volume and sentiment of comments can offer valuable insights.
- **Shares**: Shares or reposts indicate that your content is compelling enough for users to share with their followers, amplifying your reach.
- **Saves**: When users save your posts, it signals that they find your content valuable and worth revisiting. High save rates often correlate with useful, educational, or inspirational content.
- **Story Engagements**: This includes replies, shares, and interactions with stickers (polls, questions, quizzes). Tracking how users engage with your Stories can help you understand what type of content works best in this format.
- **Reels Engagements**: Monitoring likes, comments, and shares on Reels helps gauge the impact of your short-form video content.

Reach and Impressions

Understanding how many people see your content and how often it appears on their screens is crucial for assessing your visibility and brand awareness.

- **Reach**: Reach refers to the number of unique users who have seen your content. It provides a sense of how many people your posts are reaching.
- **Impressions**: Impressions measure the total number of times your content is displayed, regardless of whether it was clicked. This metric helps you understand how often your content is being shown to users.
- **Follower Growth**: Tracking the growth rate of your followers over time helps you measure your audience expansion efforts. Analyzing spikes in follower growth can also reveal which content or campaigns were particularly effective.

Traffic Metrics

If driving traffic to your website or landing page is one of your goals, tracking the following metrics is essential:

- **Link Clicks**: The number of times users click on links in your bio, Stories, or ads. This metric indicates how effectively your content drives traffic to external sites.
- **Swipe-Ups**: For accounts with over 10,000 followers, Instagram allows adding swipe-up links in Stories. Monitoring swipe-ups provides insight into how well your Stories drive traffic.

Conversion Metrics

Conversion metrics track the actions users take after interacting with your content, providing a direct link between your Instagram efforts and business results.

- **Leads Generated**: The number of leads captured through Instagram, such as email sign-ups or form submissions. This metric is crucial for measuring the effectiveness of lead-generation campaigns.
- **Sales**: Tracking sales directly attributed to Instagram, whether through Shopping tags, ads, or links in bio. This metric ties your marketing efforts to actual revenue generation.
- **Conversion Rate**: The percentage of users who complete a desired action (e.g., making a purchase, or signing up for a newsletter) after interacting with your content. A high conversion rate indicates that your audience finds your calls to action compelling.

Content Performance Metrics

Analyzing which types of content perform best can guide your content strategy and help you focus on what resonates most with your audience.

- **Top Posts**: Identifying your top-performing posts based on likes, comments, shares, and saves helps you understand what content your audience prefers.
- **Top Stories**: Reviewing which Stories receive the most engagement can provide insights into what type of ephemeral content works best.
- **Top Reels**: Monitoring the performance of your Reels, including engagement and reach, can guide your short-form video strategy.

Audience Metrics

Understanding your audience demographics and behaviors is key to creating targeted, relevant content.

- **Demographics**: Analyzing data on your followers' age, gender, location, and language helps you tailor your content to your audience's characteristics.
- **Active Times**: Knowing when your audience is most active on Instagram can help you schedule posts for maximum visibility and engagement.

Sentiment Analysis

Beyond quantitative metrics, understanding the sentiment of your audience towards your brand and content can provide deeper insights.

- **Sentiment of Comments**: Analyzing the tone and sentiment of comments on your posts helps you gauge your audience's feelings and reactions.
- **Mentions and Tags**: Monitoring how users mention and tag your brand in their posts and Stories provides insight into your brand's perception and user-generated content.

Tracking these key metrics is crucial for evaluating the success of your Instagram marketing efforts. By consistently monitoring engagement, reach, traffic, conversion, content performance, audience demographics, and sentiment, you can make data-driven decisions that enhance your strategy. Regularly reviewing these metrics allows you to identify trends, understand your audience better, and optimize your content for maximum impact. With a clear understanding of these KPIs, you can confidently navigate the dynamic world of Instagram marketing and achieve your goals.

Chapter 2: Setting Up Your Business Profile

Creating a strong foundation is crucial for successful Instagram marketing, and this starts with setting up your business profile. Your Instagram profile serves as the face of your brand on the platform, offering potential customers their first impression of your business. This chapter will guide you through the steps to establish an effective business profile, from initial setup to optimization strategies that ensure you make the most of Instagram's features.

1. Converting to a Business Account

Before diving into profile setup, it's essential to convert your personal Instagram account to a business account, if you haven't already. A business account provides access to valuable tools and insights that are not available on personal accounts.

Steps to Convert:

- **Go to Settings**: Open your Instagram app, go to your profile, and tap the three lines in the top-right corner to access the menu. Select "Settings."
- **Switch to Professional Account**: In the Settings menu, select "Account," then tap "Switch to Professional Account."
- **Choose Business**: Select "Business" as your account type. You may also choose "Creator" if you're an influencer or content creator, but "Business" is typically best for companies and brands.

- **Connect to Facebook**: Instagram will prompt you to connect your account to a Facebook Page. This step is optional but recommended as it allows for easier ad management and additional features.
- **Complete Your Profile**: Follow the prompts to add business details, such as your business category and contact information.

2. Optimizing Your Profile

Once you have a business account, the next step is to optimize your profile to make a strong first impression and provide essential information about your business.

Profile Picture

Your profile picture is one of the first things users see. It should be recognizable and reflect your brand identity.

- **Use Your Logo**: A clear, high-resolution version of your logo is ideal for brand recognition.
- **Keep It Simple**: Ensure the image is clear and not overly complicated, as it will be displayed as a small circle.

Username and Display Name

Your username (handle) and display name are crucial for searchability.

- **Username**: Keep it consistent with your other social media handles and easy to remember. If your exact business name is taken, consider adding an underscore or a descriptive word (e.g., @YourBrandOfficial).
- **Display Name**: Use your full business name for the display name to make it easy for users to find you.

Bio

Your bio is a short but vital section where you can convey key information about your business.

- **Describe Your Business**: Clearly state what your business does and what makes it unique. Use concise, engaging language.
- **Include Keywords**: Incorporate relevant keywords to improve searchability.
- **Add a Call-to-Action**: Encourage users to take specific actions, such as visiting your website, signing up for a newsletter, or checking out a promotion.
- **Use Emojis Sparingly**: Emojis can help break up text and convey personality but use them judiciously to maintain professionalism.

Contact Information

Make it easy for users to contact you.

- **Email and Phone**: Add your business email and phone number. These will appear as clickable buttons on your profile.
- **Location**: If you have a physical location, add your address to help local customers find you.

Link in Bio

Instagram allows you to include one clickable link in your bio. Use this strategically to drive traffic to your most important content.

- **Website**: Link to your homepage, a specific landing page, or a current promotion.
- **Link Aggregators**: Consider using tools like Linktree or Later's Linkin.bio to create a single link that directs users to a page with multiple links to various destinations.

Highlights

Instagram Highlights allow you to showcase Stories on your profile permanently. This is a great way to feature important content.

- **Create Highlights**: Organize your Stories into Highlights such as "Products," "Testimonials," "Behind the Scenes," and "FAQs."
- **Design Covers**: Use custom highlight covers to maintain a cohesive look and feel for your profile.

3. Utilizing Instagram Features

Instagram offers a variety of features that can enhance your business profile and engagement with followers.

Instagram Shop

If you sell products, setting up an Instagram Shop can significantly boost your sales.

- **Set Up Shop**: Ensure you meet Instagram's eligibility requirements and set up your shop through Facebook Commerce Manager.
- **Tag Products**: Once your shop is set up, you can tag products in your posts and Stories, making it easy for users to purchase directly from Instagram.

Action Buttons

Instagram allows you to add action buttons to your profile to facilitate specific user actions.

- **Available Options**: Add buttons like "Order Food," "Book Now," or "Reserve" if they are relevant to your business.
- **Integration**: These buttons integrate with third-party services, making the process seamless for users.

Analytics and Insights

One of the significant advantages of a business account is access to Instagram Insights, which provides detailed analytics about your profile's performance.

- **Track Metrics**: Monitor metrics such as follower growth, post engagement, reach, and impressions.
- **Analyze Data**: Use this data to understand your audience's behavior, refine your content strategy, and improve your overall performance.

Instagram Stories and Reels

Leverage Instagram's dynamic content formats to engage your audience creatively.

- **Stories**: Use Stories for real-time updates, behind-the-scenes content, polls, and questions to interact directly with your followers.
- **Reels**: Create engaging, short-form videos to showcase your products, share tutorials, and participate in trending challenges to boost your reach.

Setting up and optimizing your Instagram business profile is the first step towards effective Instagram marketing. By converting to a business account, optimizing every element of your profile, and utilizing

Instagram's powerful features, you create a strong foundation that attracts and engages your target audience. With a well-crafted profile, you not only make a great first impression but also ensure that your business is positioned to take full advantage of everything Instagram has to offer.

2.1 Creating and Optimizing Your Business Profile

A well-crafted and optimized business profile is essential for leveraging Instagram's full potential. This section will guide you through the process of creating and optimizing your business profile, ensuring that it effectively represents your brand and attracts your target audience.

Setting Up Your Business Profile

Step 1: Download and Install the Instagram App

If you haven't already, download the Instagram app from the App Store (iOS) or Google Play Store (Android).

Step 2: Sign Up or Log In

Open the app and either sign up for a new account or log in to an existing one. If you already have a personal account, you can easily convert it to a business account.

Step 3: Convert to a Business Account

- **Go to Settings**: Tap the profile icon in the bottom right corner, then tap the three horizontal lines in the top right corner. Select "Settings."
- **Switch to Professional Account**: In the Settings menu, tap "Account," then select "Switch to Professional Account."
- **Choose Business**: Choose "Business" and follow the prompts to add your business details, such as category and contact information.
- **Connect to Facebook (Optional)**: If you have a Facebook Page for your business, connect it to your Instagram account for additional features and streamlined ad management.

Optimizing Your Profile

Profile Picture

Your profile picture is a critical aspect of your brand identity on Instagram. Here are some tips for selecting the right image:

- **Use a High-Quality Logo**: A clear, high-resolution version of your logo is ideal for brand recognition.
- **Keep It Simple**: Ensure the image is not overly complicated, as it will be displayed in a small circle. Simplicity helps with recognition.

Username and Display Name

Your username and display name are important for searchability and brand consistency.

- **Username**: Choose a username that is consistent with your brand's other social media handles. If your exact business name is unavailable, consider adding an underscore or a descriptive word (e.g., @YourBrand_Official).
- **Display Name**: Use your full business name in the display name to make it easy for users to find you.

Bio

Your bio is a brief but vital section that should communicate key information about your business.

- **Clear Description**: Summarize what your business does and what makes it unique in a few sentences.
- **Keywords**: Incorporate relevant keywords to improve searchability.
- **Call-to-Action**: Encourage users to take specific actions, such as visiting your website, signing up for a newsletter, or checking out a promotion.
- **Emojis**: Use emojis to break up text and convey personality, but keep it professional and not overdone.

Contact Information

Make it easy for users to contact you directly from your profile.

- **Email and Phone**: Add your business email and phone number. These will appear as clickable buttons on your profile.
- **Location**: If your business has a physical location, include the address to help local customers find you.

Link in Bio

Instagram allows one clickable link in your bio. Use this strategically to drive traffic to your most important content.

- **Website**: Link to your homepage, a specific landing page, or a current promotion.
- **Link Aggregators**: Consider using tools like Linktree or Later's Linkin.bio to create a single link that directs users to a page with multiple links to various destinations.

Highlights

Highlights allow you to feature Stories permanently on your profile. This is a great way to showcase important content.

- **Create Highlights**: Organize your Stories into Highlights such as "Products," "Testimonials," "Behind the Scenes," and "FAQs."
- **Design Covers**: Use custom highlight covers to maintain a cohesive look and feel for your profile.

Utilizing Instagram Features

Instagram Shop

If you sell products, setting up an Instagram Shop can significantly boost your sales.

- **Set Up Shop**: Ensure you meet Instagram's eligibility requirements and set up your shop through Facebook Commerce Manager.
- **Tag Products**: Once your shop is set up, tag products in your posts and Stories, making it easy for users to purchase directly from Instagram.

Action Buttons

Instagram allows you to add action buttons to your profile to facilitate specific user actions.

- **Available Options**: Add buttons like "Order Food," "Book Now," or "Reserve" if they are relevant to your business.

- **Integration**: These buttons integrate with third-party services, making the process seamless for users.

Analytics and Insights

One of the significant advantages of a business account is access to Instagram Insights, which provides detailed analytics about your profile's performance.

- **Track Metrics**: Monitor metrics such as follower growth, post engagement, reach, and impressions.
- **Analyze Data**: Use this data to understand your audience's behavior, refine your content strategy, and improve your overall performance.

Best Practices for Profile Optimization

To ensure your profile is as effective as possible, follow these best practices:

- **Consistency**: Maintain a consistent brand voice and aesthetic across all elements of your profile, including your bio, profile picture, and highlights.
- **Regular Updates**: Keep your profile updated with current information and fresh content. Regularly review and revise your bio, contact details, and highlights.

- **Engagement**: Actively engage with your audience by responding to comments and direct messages. Encourage interaction by asking questions and using interactive features like polls and questions in Stories.
- **Visual Appeal**: Ensure your profile is visually appealing. Use high-quality images and videos, and maintain a consistent color scheme and style.

Creating and optimizing your Instagram business profile is a critical step in building a strong online presence. By following the steps outlined in this section, you can create a professional, engaging profile that accurately represents your brand and attracts your target audience. A well-optimized profile not only makes a great first impression but also sets the stage for successful marketing campaigns on Instagram.

2.2 Crafting an Engaging Bio and Profile Picture

Your Instagram bio and profile picture are the cornerstones of your business profile. They are often the first things potential followers see and play a crucial role in making a lasting impression. This section will guide you through the process of crafting an engaging bio and selecting a compelling profile picture that effectively represents your brand.

Crafting an Engaging Bio

Your bio is a brief yet powerful tool to communicate your brand's identity, values, and purpose. It should be clear, concise, and compelling.

Elements of a Strong Bio

1. Clear Description:

- **Who You Are**: Start with a brief introduction of your business. This could be a tagline or a concise summary of what you do.
- **What You Offer**: Highlight your products, services, or unique value proposition. Make sure this is easily understandable at a glance.

2. Keywords:

- **Relevance**: Use keywords relevant to your industry and business. This improves your profile's searchability on Instagram.
- **SEO**: Think about what terms your potential customers might use to find a business like yours and include them naturally in your bio.

3. Call-to-Action (CTA):

- **Engagement**: Encourage users to take a specific action, such as visiting your website, signing up for a newsletter, or checking out your latest products.
- **Links**: Direct them to your website or a specific landing page using the link in your bio. Phrases like "Shop Now," "Learn More," or "Sign Up" can be effective.

4. Emojis:

- **Visual Appeal**: Use emojis to add personality and break up text, making your bio more visually appealing.
- **Sparingly**: While emojis can make your bio more engaging, use them sparingly to maintain professionalism.

Bio Examples

- **Retail Business**: " Trendy Apparel for Every Occasion | New Arrivals Every Week | Free Shipping on Orders Over $50 | NYC | ↓ Shop Our Collection"
- **Service Provider**: "Helping You Build Your Dream Home | Expert Renovations & Interior Design | 20+ Years of Experience | Contact Us for a Free Consultation | ↓ Get a Quote"
- **Food Blogger**: "Delicious Recipes & Food Inspiration | Daily Meal Ideas | Author of 'Cooking with Love' | Available Worldwide | ↓Try Our Latest Recipe"

Selecting a Compelling Profile Picture

Your profile picture is a visual representation of your brand and should be easily recognizable and professional.

Best Practices for Profile Pictures

1. Use Your Logo:

- **Brand Recognition**: A clear, high-resolution version of your logo is ideal for maintaining brand consistency and recognition.
- **Simplicity**: Ensure the logo is simple and not overly detailed, as it will be displayed in a small circle.

2. High Quality:

- **Resolution**: Use a high-quality image to ensure it looks good on all devices.
- **Clarity**: Avoid images that are blurry or pixelated. A clean, sharp image conveys professionalism.

3. Consistency Across Platforms:

- **Unified Brand Image**: Use the same profile picture across all social media platforms to build a cohesive brand image.
- **Ease of Recognition**: This makes it easier for followers to recognize your brand regardless of the platform.

Colors and Design:

- **Brand Colors**: Use your brand colors to maintain visual consistency.

- **Contrast**: Ensure there is enough contrast in the image so that it stands out and is easily recognizable even at a small size.

Putting It All Together

Combining an engaging bio with a compelling profile picture creates a strong and cohesive brand presence on Instagram. Here's a quick checklist to ensure you have everything covered:

Profile Picture:

- High-resolution image
- Clear and simple logo or recognizable brand image
- Consistent with other social media platforms
- Properly sized and cropped

Bio:

- Clear and concise description of your business
- Relevant keywords for improved searchability
- Effective call-to-action
- Sparing use of emojis for visual appeal

Your Instagram bio and profile picture are fundamental elements of your business profile. By crafting a bio that communicates your brand's value and selecting a profile picture that is both professional and recognizable, you set a strong foundation for your Instagram presence. These elements work together to create a memorable first impression, attract your target audience, and encourage engagement. Take the time to refine these components, and you'll be well on your way to establishing a successful Instagram business profile.

2.3 Utilizing Instagram Business Tools and Insights

Once your Instagram business profile is set up and optimized, it's time to leverage the powerful tools and insights available to enhance your marketing efforts. Instagram offers a range of features designed specifically for businesses, providing valuable data and functionalities that can help you grow your audience, engage with followers, and measure your success. This section will explore these tools and how to use them effectively.

Instagram Insights

Instagram Insights is a built-in analytics tool that provides detailed information about your followers, post-performance, and overall engagement. Accessing and understanding these insights can help you refine your strategy and make data-driven decisions.

Accessing Instagram Insights

- **Navigate to Insights**: Go to your profile and tap the three horizontal lines in the top right corner. Select "Insights" from the menu.

- **Overview**: The Insights dashboard provides an overview of your account's performance, including metrics for content, activity, and audience.

Key Metrics to Track

1. Content Insights:

- **Past Performance**: View metrics such as likes, comments, shares, and saves for individual posts.
- **Stories and Reels**: Analyze the performance of your Stories and Reels, including views, replies, and interactions.
- **Top Posts**: Identify your most engaging posts to understand what type of content resonates with your audience.

2. Activity Insights:

- **Interactions**: Track profile visits, website clicks, and call-to-action button clicks.
- **Discovery**: Measure reach and impressions to understand how many unique users see your content and how often it appears on their screens.

3. Audience Insights:

- **Follower Demographics**: Analyze data on your followers' age, gender, location, and active times.

- **Growth**: Monitor your follower growth over time and identify trends or spikes in follower acquisition.

Using Insights to Inform Strategy

- **Content Optimization**: Use insights to determine which types of content perform best and tailor your future posts accordingly.
- **Posting Schedule**: Identify the times when your followers are most active and schedule your posts to maximize engagement.
- **Audience Understanding**: Gain a deeper understanding of your audience demographics and interests to create more targeted and relevant content.

Instagram Business Tools

In addition to Insights, Instagram offers several tools designed to help businesses promote their products and engage with their audience effectively.

Instagram Shopping

Instagram Shopping allows businesses to create a virtual storefront on their profile, making it easy for users to browse and purchase products directly from the app.

1. Set Up Instagram Shop:

- **Eligibility**: Ensure your business meets Instagram's eligibility requirements for setting up a shop.
- **Commerce Manager**: Use Facebook Commerce Manager to set up your shop, add products, and manage your catalog.
- **Product Tagging**: Tag products in your posts and Stories to enable users to shop directly from your content.

2. Shopping Features:

- **Shop Tab**: Add a "View Shop" button to your profile, allowing users to access your storefront easily.
- **Product Stickers**: Use product stickers in Stories to showcase individual items and provide direct links to purchase.

Action Buttons

Instagram allows businesses to add action buttons to their profile, enabling users to take specific actions such as booking an appointment, placing an order, or making a reservation.

1. Add Action Buttons:

Navigate to Edit Profile: Go to your profile and tap "Edit Profile."

Select Action Buttons: Under "Contact Options," choose the relevant action buttons for your business.

Integrate Services: Link these buttons to third-party services like OpenTable, Resy, or Eventbrite to streamline the process for users.

Instagram Ads

Instagram Ads are a powerful tool for reaching a broader audience and promoting your business. With various ad formats and targeting options, you can create effective campaigns tailored to your specific goals.

1. **Ad Formats:**

- **Photo Ads**: High-quality images that appear in users' feeds.
- **Video Ads**: Engaging videos up to 60 seconds long.
- **Carousel Ads**: Multiple images or videos that users can swipe through.
- **Story Ads**: Full-screen ads that appear between users' Stories.
- **Reel Ads**: Short, engaging video ads in the Reels section.

2. **Targeting Options:**

- **Demographics**: Target users based on age, gender, location, and language.
- **Interests**: Reach users based on their interests and behaviors.
- **Custom Audiences**: Target users who have interacted with your business before or upload your customer lists.

- **Lookalike Audiences**: Find new users who are similar to your existing customers.

3. Creating Ads:

- **Use Ads Manager**: Create and manage your Instagram ads through Facebook Ads Manager.
- **Set Objectives**: Define your campaign objectives, such as brand awareness, traffic, or conversions.
- **Monitor Performance**: Track the performance of your ads using Ads Manager and adjust your strategy as needed.

Utilizing Instagram's business tools and insights is crucial for maximizing the effectiveness of your marketing efforts on the platform. By leveraging Instagram Insights, you can gain valuable data to inform your strategy and optimize your content. Instagram Shopping, action buttons, and ads provide powerful functionalities to engage your audience and drive business results. Incorporating these tools into your Instagram strategy will help you create a more dynamic and successful presence, ultimately leading to greater brand visibility, engagement, and growth.

2.4 Integrating Contact Options and Call-to-Actions

Effective communication with your audience and guiding them toward desired actions are critical aspects of Instagram marketing. Integrating clear contact options and compelling call-to-actions (CTAs) into your profile and content can significantly enhance user engagement and drive business results. This section will explain how to set up contact options and craft effective CTAs to maximize your Instagram marketing efforts.

Integrating Contact Options

Making it easy for users to contact your business directly from your Instagram profile can improve customer service and facilitate transactions.

Adding Contact Information

1. Email Address:

- **Visibility**: Add your business email address to your profile so users can contact you with inquiries.
- **Setup**: Go to "Edit Profile," then tap "Contact Options" and enter your business email address. This will create an "Email" button on your profile.

2. Phone Number:

- **Accessibility**: Providing a phone number allows users to call or text your business directly.
- **Setup**: In the "Contact Options" section, enter your business phone number. This will add a "Call" or "Text" button to your profile.

3. Physical Address:

- **Local Businesses**: If you have a physical location, include your address to help local customers find you.
- **Setup**: Enter your address in the "Contact Options" section. This will display a "Directions" button on your profile.

4. Action Buttons:

- **Integration**: Add action buttons for specific tasks like booking appointments, ordering food, or making reservations.
- **Setup**: In the "Edit Profile" section, select "Action Buttons" and choose from the available options. These buttons integrate with third-party services such as OpenTable, Resy, or Grubhub.

Crafting Effective Call-to-Actions (CTAs)

CTAs are essential for guiding your audience towards specific actions, such as visiting your website, making a purchase, or following your account.

Best Practices for CTAs

1. Clarity and Simplicity:

- **Direct Language**: Use clear and direct language that tells users exactly what you want them to do (e.g., "Shop Now," "Learn More," "Sign Up").
- **Brevity**: Keep your CTAs short and to the point to ensure they are easily understood.

2. Action-Oriented:

- **Strong Verbs**: Start your CTAs with strong action verbs to create a sense of urgency and encourage immediate action (e.g., "Discover," "Join," "Download").
- **Value Proposition**: Highlight the benefit of taking the action, such as exclusive discounts, free resources, or new product releases.

3. Placement:

- **Profile Bio**: Include a CTA in your bio to direct users to your most important link. Use phrases like "Check out our latest collection" or "Get a free consultation."
- **Posts and Stories**: Incorporate CTAs in your captions and Stories to drive engagement. Use stickers like "Swipe Up" in Stories (available for accounts with 10,000+ followers) to provide a direct link.

Consistency:

- **Brand Voice**: Ensure your CTAs are consistent with your brand voice and messaging.
- **Repetition**: Repeat CTAs across different posts and Stories to reinforce the action you want users to take.

Examples of Effective CTAs

1. For E-Commerce:

- **Post Caption**: " New arrivals just in! Shop the latest trends now. Tap the link in our bio to start shopping. #NewArrivals #ShopNow"
- **Story**: Use the "Swipe Up" feature with the text "Swipe up to shop our new collection!"

2. For Service Providers:

- **Post Caption**: "Ready to transform your space? Book a free consultation with our expert designers today. Link in bio. #InteriorDesign #FreeConsultation"
- **Story**: Use a "Questions" sticker with the text "Need design advice? Ask us anything!"

3. For Content Creators:

- **Post Caption**: "Don't miss out on our latest tutorial! Learn how to create stunning visuals. Watch now via the link in our bio. #Tutorial #LearnWithUs"
- **Story**: Use the "Swipe Up" feature with the text "Swipe up to watch our latest tutorial!"

Implementing CTAs in Instagram Ads

Instagram Ads provide an excellent opportunity to reach a broader audience and drive specific actions through targeted campaigns.

1. Ad Formats:

- **Photo Ads**: Use compelling images with a strong CTA in the caption and a clickable button (e.g., "Shop Now," "Learn More").
- **Video Ads**: Include a CTA both in the video content and the accompanying text. Ensure the CTA appears early and clearly.
- **Story Ads**: Leverage the full-screen format to include a prominent CTA, such as "Swipe Up" for direct links to your website or product page.

2. Targeting and Retargeting:

- **Custom Audiences**: Target users who have previously interacted with your brand or visited your website to encourage them to complete a desired action.
- **Lookalike Audiences**: Reach new users similar to your existing customers who are likely to be interested in your offerings.

3. Performance Monitoring:

- **Track Metrics**: Use Instagram Insights and Ads Manager to monitor the performance of your ads, focusing on metrics like click-through rates (CTR), conversions, and engagement.
- **A/B Testing**: Experiment with different CTAs, ad formats, and targeting options to determine what works best for your audience.

Integrating contact options and crafting effective call-to-actions are vital components of a successful Instagram marketing strategy. By making it easy for users to contact your business and providing clear, compelling CTAs, you can enhance user engagement, drive specific actions, and ultimately achieve your marketing goals. Take advantage of Instagram's business tools and insights to refine your approach, ensuring that every interaction with your audience is purposeful and impactful.

Chapter 3: Content Strategy and Planning

Creating a successful Instagram marketing campaign requires more than just posting random photos and videos. It necessitates a well-thought-out content strategy and meticulous planning to ensure consistency, engagement, and alignment with your brand's goals. This chapter will guide you through the essential steps for developing an effective content strategy and planning your posts to maximize your reach and impact.

1. Understanding Your Audience

The foundation of any successful content strategy is a deep understanding of your audience. Knowing who your followers are and what they want to see will help you create content that resonates with them and drives engagement.

Identifying Your Target Audience

- **Demographics**: Identify key demographic information about your audience, such as age, gender, location, and language. This data can be gathered from Instagram Insights or your customer database.
- **Interests and Behaviors**: Understand what interests your audience, including hobbies, values, and lifestyle choices. Consider what kind of content they engage with on Instagram and other social media platforms.

- **Pain Points and Needs**: Identify the challenges and needs of your audience. What problems can your product or service solve for them? How can your content address these issues?

Creating Audience Personas

Develop detailed personas that represent different segments of your target audience. Each persona should include:

- **Name and Background**: Create a fictional name and brief background for the persona.
- **Demographics**: Age, gender, location, occupation, and income level.
- **Interests**: Hobbies, favorite brands, and types of content they enjoy.
- **Challenges**: Common pain points and problems they face.
- **Goals**: What they hope to achieve through your product or service.

Leveraging Instagram Insights

Instagram Insights provides valuable data about your followers and their interactions with your content. Use this tool to:

- **Track Follower Growth**: Monitor how your follower count changes over time.
- **Engagement Metrics**: Analyze likes, comments, shares, and saves to determine what type of content performs best.

- **Audience Demographics**: Review data on your followers' age, gender, location, and active times to tailor your content strategy.

2. Defining Your Content Pillars

Content pillars are the main themes or topics that your content will revolve around. They provide structure and ensure your content remains aligned with your brand's message and goals.

Identifying Your Content Pillars

- **Brand Values and Mission**: Reflect on your brand's core values and mission. What messages do you want to communicate to your audience?
- **Audience Interests**: Consider what topics resonate most with your target audience. Refer back to your audience personas for insights.
- **Product and Service Features**: Highlight the key features and benefits of your products or services.

Examples of Content Pillars

- **Educational Content**: Posts that provide valuable information, tips, and advice related to your industry or products.
- **Behind-the-scenes**: Give your audience a glimpse into the day-to-day operations of your business, including team activities and production processes.

- **Customer Stories**: Share testimonials, reviews, and success stories from your customers to build trust and social proof.
- **Promotional Content**: Highlight special offers, new product launches, and events to drive sales and engagement.
- **User-Generated Content**: Feature content created by your customers, such as photos, videos, and reviews, to foster community and authenticity.

3. Creating a Content Calendar

A content calendar helps you plan and organize your posts in advance, ensuring consistency and strategic alignment. It allows you to maintain a regular posting schedule, track important dates, and measure the effectiveness of your content.

Steps to Create a Content Calendar

- **Set Goals and Objectives**: Define what you aim to achieve with your content, such as increasing brand awareness, driving traffic, or boosting sales.
- **Determine Posting Frequency**: Decide how often you will post on Instagram. Consistency is key, so choose a frequency that you can maintain.
- **Plan Content Types**: Mix different types of content (e.g., photos, videos, Stories, Reels) to keep your feed diverse and engaging.
- **Schedule Posts**: Use a content calendar tool or a simple spreadsheet to schedule your posts in advance. Include details like post date, time, content type, caption, hashtags, and any relevant links.

- **Incorporate Key Dates**: Mark important dates such as holidays, product launches, events, and campaigns to ensure timely and relevant content.

Tools for Content Planning

- **Instagram Planner Apps**: Tools like Later, Planoly, and Buffer allow you to schedule and preview your posts, ensuring a cohesive feed.
- **Project Management Tools**: Use tools like Trello or Asana to organize your content ideas, assign tasks, and track deadlines.
- **Spreadsheets**: Create a simple content calendar using Google Sheets or Excel to keep track of your posting schedule and content details.

4. Crafting High-Quality Content

The quality of your content is crucial for capturing your audience's attention and driving engagement. High-quality content is visually appealing, informative, and aligned with your brand's message.

Tips for Creating High-Quality Content

1. Visual Aesthetics:

- **Consistent Style**: Maintain a consistent visual style, including color scheme, filters, and branding elements.

- **High-Resolution Images**: Use high-quality, high-resolution images and videos to ensure your content looks professional.
- **Composition and Lighting**: Pay attention to composition and lighting to create visually striking content.

2. Engaging Captions:

- **Compelling Headlines**: Start with a strong headline to grab attention.
- **Brand Voice**: Write in a tone that reflects your brand's personality and values.
- **Call-to-Action**: Include a clear call-to-action to encourage interaction and engagement.

3. Relevant Hashtags:

- **Industry Hashtags**: Use popular hashtags relevant to your industry to increase visibility.
- **Branded Hashtags**: Create and promote your own branded hashtags to build a community and encourage user-generated content.

4. Storytelling:

- **Narrative Approach**: Use storytelling techniques to make your content more relatable and engaging.

- **Customer Stories**: Share real stories from your customers to create an emotional connection with your audience.

5. User-Generated Content:

- **Encouragement**: Encourage your followers to create and share content related to your brand.
- **Feature UGC**: Regularly feature user-generated content on your profile to show appreciation and build community.

Tools for Content Creation

- **Photo Editing**: Use tools like Adobe Lightroom, VSCO, or Snapseed to enhance your images.
- **Graphic Design**: Create stunning graphics and visuals with tools like Canva or Adobe Spark.
- **Video Editing**: Edit your videos using apps like InShot, Adobe Premiere Rush, or Final Cut Pro.

A well-planned content strategy is essential for achieving success on Instagram. By understanding your audience, defining your content pillars, creating a content calendar, and crafting high-quality content, you can build a strong and engaging presence on the platform. Consistency, creativity, and strategic planning are key to driving engagement, building a loyal following, and achieving your business goals. Take the time to develop and refine your content strategy, and you'll be well on your way to Instagram marketing success.

3.1 Developing a Content Calendar

A content calendar is a strategic tool that helps you plan, organize, and manage your Instagram posts effectively. It ensures that your content is consistent, timely, and aligned with your marketing goals. Developing a content calendar involves several key steps, from setting your objectives to scheduling your posts. This section will guide you through the process of creating a robust content calendar for your Instagram marketing.

Setting Goals and Objectives

Before you start creating your content calendar, it's essential to define your goals and objectives. What do you want to achieve with your Instagram content? Common goals include increasing brand awareness, driving website traffic, boosting sales, or growing your follower base. Having clear objectives will help you tailor your content strategy and measure your success.

Determining Your Posting Frequency

Consistency is crucial for maintaining engagement and building a loyal audience on Instagram. Decide how often you will post, keeping in mind that the ideal frequency can vary depending on your industry and audience. While some brands may benefit from daily posts, others may find success with a few high-quality posts per week. Assess your resources and choose a posting schedule that you can maintain consistently.

Planning Content Types

Variety in content keeps your audience engaged and interested. Plan a mix of content types to ensure a dynamic and engaging feed. Consider incorporating the following content types into your calendar:

- **Photos**: High-quality images showcasing your products, services, or brand lifestyle.
- **Videos**: Engaging video content, including tutorials, behind-the-scenes, or customer testimonials.
- **Stories**: Short, ephemeral content that provides real-time updates, polls, or interactive elements.
- **Reels**: Short, creative videos that highlight trends, tips, or entertaining content.
- **Carousel Posts**: Multiple images or videos in a single post, ideal for detailed stories or product showcases.
- **IGTV**: Longer video content for in-depth tutorials, interviews, or webinars.

Scheduling Your Posts

Once you have determined your posting frequency and content types, it's time to schedule your posts. A content calendar helps you organize your posts in advance, ensuring a consistent and strategic approach. Here's how to create a content calendar:

- **Choose a Tool**: Use a content calendar tool or a simple spreadsheet to plan your posts. Tools like Google Sheets, Trello,

Asana, Later, or Planoly can help you organize and visualize your schedule.

- **Mark Key Dates**: Identify important dates such as holidays, product launches, events, or promotional campaigns. Plan content around these dates to ensure timely and relevant posts.
- **Create a Posting Schedule**: Map out your content for each day, week, or month. Include details like post date, time, content type, caption, hashtags, and any relevant links.
- **Content Themes**: Assign specific themes or content pillars to different days of the week to maintain a balanced and cohesive feed. For example, you might dedicate Mondays to motivational quotes, Wednesdays to product highlights, and Fridays to user-generated content.
- **Plan Ahead**: Schedule posts at least one month in advance to give yourself enough time to create high-quality content and make adjustments as needed.

Incorporating Flexibility

While planning is essential, it's also important to remain flexible and adaptable. The social media landscape can change quickly, and you may need to adjust your content calendar in response to current events, trending topics, or new opportunities. Regularly review and update your calendar to keep it relevant and effective.

Tools for Content Planning

Several tools can help you create and manage your content calendar efficiently:

- **Later**: A popular Instagram scheduling tool that allows you to plan, schedule, and analyze your posts.
- **Planoly**: A visual planner and scheduler for Instagram that helps you organize your feed and track performance.
- **Buffer**: A social media management tool that enables you to schedule and publish posts across multiple platforms.
- **Hootsuite**: A comprehensive social media management platform that includes scheduling, monitoring, and analytics features.
- **Trello**: A flexible project management tool that can be customized to create a content calendar with cards, lists, and due dates.

Reviewing and Adjusting Your Calendar

Regularly reviewing your content calendar is crucial for maintaining its effectiveness. Analyze the performance of your posts using Instagram Insights and other analytics tools to understand what's working and what's not. Use this data to make informed adjustments to your content strategy and calendar. Continuously optimizing your approach will help you stay relevant and achieve your marketing goals.

Developing a content calendar is a vital step in executing a successful Instagram marketing strategy. By setting clear goals, determining your posting frequency, planning diverse content types, and scheduling your posts in advance, you can maintain consistency and strategic alignment. Incorporate flexibility to adapt to changing circumstances, and use tools to streamline your planning process. Regularly review and adjust your calendar based on performance insights to ensure ongoing success and growth on Instagram.

3.2 Balancing Different Types of Content (Posts, Stories, Reels, IGTV)

A successful Instagram marketing strategy relies on balancing various types of content to keep your audience engaged and interested. Each content type on Instagram—Posts, Stories, Reels, and IGTV—serves a different purpose and caters to different audience preferences. This section will guide you on how to effectively balance these content types to create a dynamic and engaging Instagram presence.

Understanding Each Content Type

1. Posts

Standard Posts are the backbone of your Instagram presence. They appear in your followers' feeds and stay on your profile permanently unless you choose to delete them.

- **Purpose**: Showcase high-quality images and videos, share product highlights, announce updates, and provide valuable information.
- **Best Practices**: Use high-resolution visuals, engaging captions, and relevant hashtags, and tag other users or locations when appropriate.

2. Stories

Instagram Stories are ephemeral posts that disappear after 24 hours unless saved to your Highlights. They are displayed at the top of your followers' feeds.

- **Purpose**: Share real-time updates, behind-the-scenes content, quick tips, polls, Q&A sessions, and more interactive content.
- **Best Practices**: Use stickers (polls, questions, countdowns), keep the content casual and authentic, and encourage direct interaction through replies or swipe-ups (for accounts with over 10,000 followers).

3. Reels

Instagram Reels are short, engaging videos designed to be entertaining and shareable. They can be up to 60 seconds long and are featured prominently in the Explore tab.

- **Purpose**: Create viral content, participate in trends, share quick tutorials, and highlight fun or creative aspects of your brand.
- **Best Practices**: Use trending music, add text overlays, keep the content fast-paced and engaging, and include a clear call-to-action.

4. IGTV

IGTV is designed for longer video content, allowing videos up to 60 minutes (for verified accounts; and 15 minutes for others).

- **Purpose**: Share in-depth tutorials, interviews, product demonstrations, and other long-form content.
- **Best Practices**: Plan and script your videos, ensure high production quality, use engaging thumbnails, and promote your IGTV content through posts and Stories.

Balancing Content Types

To maintain a well-rounded and engaging Instagram presence, it's important to strike the right balance between these content types. Here's how to achieve that balance:

Weekly Content Mix

1. Daily Posts:

- **Frequency**: Aim for at least 3-5 posts per week.
- **Content**: Mix product highlights, customer testimonials, educational content, and promotional offers.

2. Regular Stories:

- **Frequency**: Post Stories daily or multiple times a day.
- **Content**: Share behind-the-scenes looks, quick updates, interactive elements (polls, Q&A), and user-generated content.

3. Weekly Reels:

- **Frequency**: Post at least 1-2 Reels per week.
- **Content**: Participate in trends, share quick tips, showcase fun aspects of your brand, and highlight user-generated content.

4. Bi-Weekly IGTV:

- **Frequency**: Post at least 1 IGTV video every 1-2 weeks.
- **Content**: Provide in-depth tutorials, host interviews, share longer product demonstrations, and explore topics in detail.

Content Planning Tips

- **Align with Goals**: Ensure that each piece of content aligns with your overall marketing goals, whether it's driving sales, increasing brand awareness, or fostering community engagement.
- **Variety and Consistency**: Maintain a variety of content types while posting consistently. This keeps your feed dynamic and caters to different audience preferences.
- **Repurpose Content**: Adapt content across different formats. For example, a product demo from an IGTV video can be condensed into a Reel, or highlights from a Q&A session in Stories can be shared as a post.
- **Engagement and Feedback**: Monitor engagement metrics to understand what types of content resonate most with your audience. Use feedback to adjust your content strategy accordingly.

Leveraging Each Content Type

Posts

- **Visual Storytelling**: Use posts to tell your brand's story through compelling visuals and narratives.
- **Promotional Content**: Highlight new products, services, or special offers.
- **Evergreen Content**: Share content that remains relevant over time, such as tips, tutorials, and FAQs.

Stories

- **Interactive Elements**: Use Stories for interactive content like polls, quizzes, and Q&A sessions to engage your audience.
- **Time-Sensitive Updates**: Share flash sales, limited-time offers, and event updates.
- **Personal Touch**: Show the human side of your brand with behind-the-scenes content and day-to-day activities.

Reels

- **Trend Participation**: Join trending challenges and use popular music to increase visibility.
- **Quick Tips**: Share bite-sized, valuable information that's easy to consume and share.

- **Entertaining Content**: Create fun and creative videos that entertain and captivate your audience.

IGTV

- **Long-Form Content**: Dive deep into topics that require more time to explain, such as detailed tutorials or interviews.
- **Series Format**: Create a series of related videos to build anticipation and keep viewers coming back for more.
- **Cross-Promotion**: Promote your IGTV videos through posts and Stories to drive more views.

Balancing different types of content on Instagram is crucial for maintaining an engaging and dynamic presence. By understanding the unique purposes and best practices for Posts, Stories, Reels, and IGTV, you can create a diverse content strategy that appeals to various audience preferences. Plan a content mix that aligns with your marketing goals, repurpose content across formats, and regularly review your performance to optimize your approach. This balanced strategy will help you maximize your reach, foster engagement, and achieve sustained growth on Instagram.

3.3 Crafting High-Quality Visual Content

Visual content is the heart of Instagram marketing. With millions of users scrolling through their feeds every day, capturing their attention with high-quality visuals is essential for standing out and engaging your audience. This section will explore how to craft visually appealing content that grabs attention, tells your brand story, and drives engagement on Instagram.

Importance of High-Quality Visuals

- **First Impression**: Your visuals are the first thing users see when they encounter your brand on Instagram. High-quality images and videos leave a positive impression and draw users in.
- **Brand Identity**: Visuals play a crucial role in shaping your brand identity and communicating your brand values and personality to your audience.
- **Engagement**: Compelling visuals are more likely to capture users' attention and encourage them to like, comment, and share your content, driving engagement and visibility.

Tips for Crafting High-Quality Visual Content

1. Invest in Photography and Videography

- **Professional Equipment**: Use high-quality cameras, lenses, and lighting equipment to capture crisp, clear images and videos.
- **Composition**: Pay attention to composition, framing, and perspective to create visually pleasing shots. Experiment with different angles and perspectives to add depth and interest to your visuals.

2. Maintain Brand Consistency

- **Visual Style Guide**: Establish a visual style guide that outlines your brand colors, fonts, and aesthetic preferences. Ensure consistency across all your visual content to reinforce your brand identity.
- **Branded Elements**: Incorporate branded elements such as logos, colors, and graphics into your visuals to create a cohesive and recognizable brand presence on Instagram.

3. Tell a Story

- **Narrative Approach**: Use visuals to tell a story and evoke emotions in your audience. Whether it's showcasing your brand journey, highlighting customer stories, or sharing behind-the-scenes moments, storytelling adds depth and authenticity to your content.
- **Emotional Appeal**: Connect with your audience on an emotional level by eliciting feelings of joy, excitement, or nostalgia through your visuals. Emotionally resonant content is more likely to leave a lasting impression and foster stronger connections with your audience.

4. Enhance Visual Appeal

- **Editing Tools**: Use photo and video editing tools to enhance the visual appeal of your content. Adjust brightness, contrast, saturation, and sharpness to achieve the desired look and feel.

- **Filters and Effects**: Experiment with filters and effects to add personality and flair to your visuals. Choose filters that align with your brand aesthetic and enhance the overall mood of your content.

5. Optimize for Instagram

- **Aspect Ratio**: Ensure your images and videos are optimized for Instagram's platform. Use the recommended aspect ratios (e.g., 4:5 for portrait images, 1:1 for square images) to ensure your content displays properly in users' feeds.
- **Captions and Hashtags**: Pair your visuals with compelling captions and relevant hashtags to provide context and increase discoverability. Use captions to add value, share stories, and encourage engagement with your audience.

6. Test and Iterate

- **Analytical Insights**: Monitor the performance of your visual content using Instagram Insights and other analytics tools. Pay attention to metrics such as engagement rate, reach, and impressions to identify what types of visuals resonate most with your audience.
- **A/B Testing**: Experiment with different types of visual content, styles, and formats to see what works best for your audience. Use A/B testing to compare the performance of different visuals and refine your content strategy accordingly.

Tools for Creating High-Quality Visual Content

- **Adobe Creative Cloud**: Suite of professional design and editing tools including Photoshop, Lightroom, and Premiere Pro for creating and editing images and videos.
- **Canva**: User-friendly graphic design platform with customizable templates and a wide range of design elements for creating stunning visuals.
- **VSCO**: Photo editing app with a variety of filters and editing tools to enhance the visual quality of your images.
- **InShot**: Video editing app for creating and editing high-quality videos with features like trimming, cropping, and adding music and effects.
- **Unsplash** and **Pexels**: Platforms offering a vast library of high-quality, royalty-free images and videos for use in your visual content.

Crafting high-quality visual content is essential for success on Instagram. By investing in photography and videography, maintaining brand consistency, telling compelling stories, enhancing visual appeal, and optimizing for the platform, you can create visually stunning content that captivates your audience and drives engagement. Experiment with different tools and techniques, monitor performance metrics, and continually refine your approach to create a visually cohesive and impactful Instagram presence that resonates with your audience.

3.4 Writing Compelling Captions and Using Hashtags Effectively

Captions and hashtags play a crucial role in enhancing the impact and reach of your Instagram posts. A well-crafted caption can complement your visual content, tell your brand story, and encourage engagement, while strategic use of hashtags can increase discoverability and attract new followers. This section will explore how to write compelling captions and use hashtags effectively to maximize the effectiveness of your Instagram marketing efforts.

Writing Compelling Captions

1. Know Your Audience

Understanding: Tailor your captions to resonate with your target audience. Consider their preferences, interests, and communication styles.

2. Tell a Story

Engagement: Use captions to tell stories that complement your visual content. Share anecdotes, behind-the-scenes moments, or personal insights to connect with your audience on a deeper level.

3. Add Value

Informative: Provide valuable information, tips, or advice related to your content or industry. Offer solutions to common problems or answer frequently asked questions.

4. Use Emotion

Emotive Language: Elicit emotions such as joy, curiosity, or inspiration through your captions. Emotionally resonant content is more likely to capture attention and encourage engagement.

5. Include a Call-to-Action (CTA)

Engagement: Encourage interaction with your audience by including a clear call-to-action in your captions. Ask questions, invite comments, or prompt users to share their thoughts or experiences.

Using Hashtags Effectively

1. Choose Relevant Hashtags

Relevance: Select hashtags that are relevant to your content, target audience, and industry. Use a mix of broad and niche hashtags to increase visibility and attract the right audience.

2. Research Popular Hashtags

Trending Topics: Stay updated on trending topics and popular hashtags within your niche. Use tools like Instagram Explore, Trendsmap, or hashtag-tracking apps to identify relevant trends.

3. Mix Hashtag Types

Variety: Use a combination of different hashtag types, including general, niche-specific, branded, and community hashtags. This diversifies your reach and increases the likelihood of discovery by different user groups.

4. Limit Hashtag Count

Relevance: Avoid overloading your captions with hashtags. Stick to a moderate number of hashtags (usually 5-10) that are highly relevant to your content. Quality over quantity is key.

5. Hide Hashtags

Aesthetic Appeal: Keep your captions clean and visually appealing by hiding hashtags. Place them at the end of your caption or in a separate comment to avoid cluttering your post.

Tools for Hashtag Research

- **Instagram Explore**: Explore trending topics and popular hashtags within your niche directly on the Instagram app.
- **Hashtagify**: Research and analyze hashtag performance, popularity, and related hashtags across different social media platforms.
- **TagBlender**: Discover relevant hashtags and create custom hashtag sets based on your content and industry.
- **RiteTag**: Get real-time hashtag suggestions and insights to optimize your hashtag strategy for maximum visibility.

Writing compelling captions and using hashtags effectively are essential components of a successful Instagram marketing strategy. By crafting captions that resonate with your audience, tell compelling stories, and include clear calls to action, you can increase engagement and foster stronger connections with your followers. Similarly, strategic use of hashtags can enhance discoverability, attract new followers, and amplify the reach of your content. Experiment with different caption styles, monitor hashtag performance, and continuously refine your approach to optimize your Instagram presence and achieve your marketing goals.

Chapter 4: Growing Your Audience

Growing your audience on Instagram is a key objective for many businesses and influencers. A larger audience means increased brand visibility, engagement, and potential for conversions. In this chapter, we will explore effective strategies and techniques to help you attract new followers, engage with your audience, and cultivate a thriving community on Instagram.

1. Understanding Your Target Audience

Before you can effectively grow your audience, you need to understand who your target audience is. Take the time to research and identify the demographics, interests, and behaviors of your ideal followers. Use tools like Instagram Insights, audience surveys, and social listening to gather valuable insights. Understanding your audience will allow you to tailor your content and engagement strategies to resonate with their preferences and needs.

2. Creating Compelling Content

Compelling content is the cornerstone of audience growth on Instagram. Develop a content strategy that showcases your brand personality, values, and offerings in a visually appealing and engaging way. Focus on creating high-quality images and videos that captivate your audience's attention and encourage them to like, comment, and share. Experiment with different content formats, storytelling techniques, and visual styles to keep your audience interested and coming back for more.

3. Engaging with Your Audience

Engagement is key to fostering a strong connection with your audience and encouraging loyalty and advocacy. Take the time to actively engage with your followers by responding to comments, liking and sharing user-generated content, and participating in conversations. Show appreciation for your audience's support and contributions, and make them feel valued and heard. Building genuine relationships with your followers will encourage them to become loyal fans and brand ambassadors.

4. Leveraging Hashtags and Explore Page

Hashtags are powerful tools for increasing your content's discoverability and reaching new audiences on Instagram. Research relevant hashtags within your niche and incorporate them strategically into your posts to expand your reach. Additionally, aim to get featured on the Explore page by creating high-quality, engaging content that resonates with a wide audience. The Explore page is a valuable source of organic reach and can help expose your brand to new users who may be interested in your content.

5. Collaborating with Influencers and Partners

Collaborating with influencers and brand partners is an effective way to tap into new audiences and accelerate your audience growth on Instagram. Identify influencers and brands that align with your values and target audience, and explore collaboration opportunities such as sponsored posts, takeovers, or joint giveaways. Leveraging the reach and credibility of influencers and partners can help you gain exposure to their followers and attract new followers who are interested in your products or services.

6. Running Contests and Giveaways

Contests and giveaways are fun and engaging ways to incentivize audience participation and attract new followers on Instagram. Create exciting and relevant giveaways that encourage users to like, comment, share, and tag their friends to enter. Promote your contest across your social channels and partner with influencers or brands to amplify reach. Running contests and giveaways not only increases engagement and brand awareness but also provides valuable user-generated content and opportunities for future collaborations.

7. Analyzing and Iterating

As you implement various strategies to grow your audience on Instagram, it's important to regularly monitor and analyze your performance metrics. Use Instagram Insights and other analytics tools to track key metrics such as follower growth, engagement rate, reach, and impressions. Identify what content resonates most with your audience and which strategies are driving the best results. Use this data to iterate and optimize your approach, refining your content, engagement, and growth strategies over time to achieve sustainable audience growth and success on Instagram.

Growing your audience on Instagram requires a combination of strategic planning, compelling content creation, active engagement, and continuous optimization. By understanding your target audience, creating high-quality content, engaging authentically with your followers, leveraging hashtags and the Explore page, collaborating with influencers and partners, running contests and giveaways, and analyzing performance metrics, you can attract new followers, build a loyal community, and achieve your business goals on Instagram. Stay adaptable, experiment with different tactics, and stay true to your brand identity to foster sustainable growth and success on the platform.

4.1 Identifying and Understanding Your Target Audience

Understanding your target audience is fundamental to the success of your Instagram marketing efforts. By identifying and understanding the demographics, interests, and behaviors of your ideal followers, you can tailor your content and engagement strategies to resonate with their preferences and needs. In this section, we will explore effective techniques for identifying and understanding your target audience on Instagram.

1. Conduct Market Research

Start by conducting thorough market research to gain insights into your target audience. Analyze your existing customer base, survey your followers, and study your competitors' followers to identify common characteristics and preferences. Use tools like Instagram Insights, Google Analytics, and social listening platforms to gather valuable data on demographics, interests, and online behavior.

2. Define Buyer Personas

Develop detailed buyer personas that represent different segments of your target audience. Each persona should include demographic information such as age, gender, location, occupation, and income level, as well as psychographic factors such as interests, hobbies, values, and pain points. Creating personas helps you humanize your audience and tailor your marketing efforts to meet their specific needs and preferences.

3. Analyze Instagram Insights

Utilize Instagram Insights to gain valuable data about your existing audience and their interactions with your content. Explore metrics such as follower demographics, engagement rate, reach, impressions, and top-performing posts to understand who your audience is and what type of content they respond to best. Use this data to refine your content strategy and optimize your approach for maximum impact.

4. Monitor Social Listening

Engage in social listening to monitor conversations and trends related to your industry or niche on Instagram. Pay attention to hashtags, mentions, and comments related to your brand or relevant topics to gain insights into your audience's interests, preferences, and pain points. Use these insights to inform your content strategy, identify opportunities for engagement, and stay ahead of emerging trends.

5. Seek Feedback and Input

Actively seek feedback and input from your audience to better understand their needs and preferences. Encourage comments, messages, and user-generated content, and respond promptly and authentically to engage in conversations with your followers. Conduct polls, surveys, or Q&A sessions to gather insights directly from your audience and use this feedback to refine your marketing strategy and content approach.

6. Test and Iterate

Continuously test and iterate your targeting strategies to refine your understanding of your target audience and improve the effectiveness of your Instagram marketing efforts. Experiment with different content formats, messaging tones, and targeting parameters to see what resonates most with your audience. Analyze the results of your tests and make data-driven decisions to optimize your approach and achieve better outcomes over time.

Identifying and understanding your target audience is essential for success on Instagram. By conducting market research, defining buyer personas, analyzing Instagram Insights, monitoring social listening, seeking feedback and input, and continuously testing and iterating your targeting strategies, you can gain valuable insights into who your audience is and what they want. Use this knowledge to tailor your content, engagement, and marketing strategies to meet the needs and preferences of your target audience, ultimately driving engagement, loyalty, and growth on Instagram.

4.2 Strategies for Organic Growth

Organic growth on Instagram refers to the process of attracting and engaging followers through unpaid, non-promotional activities. While paid advertising can be effective for reaching new audiences, organic growth focuses on building a loyal and engaged following through authentic interactions and compelling content. In this section, we will explore effective strategies for achieving organic growth on Instagram.

1. Create High-Quality Content Consistently

Consistent and high-quality content is the foundation of organic growth on Instagram. Develop a content strategy that resonates with your target audience and showcases your brand personality, values, and offerings. Use a mix of visually appealing images, engaging videos, and compelling captions to capture your audience's attention and encourage them to like, comment, and share your content. Aim to post regularly and maintain a consistent aesthetic to keep your followers engaged and coming back for more.

2. Engage Authentically with Your Audience

Authentic engagement is key to fostering a strong connection with your audience and building a loyal following on Instagram. Take the time to respond to comments, messages, and mentions promptly and authentically. Show appreciation for your followers' support and contributions, and engage in genuine conversations to build rapport and trust. Use Instagram Stories, polls, and Q&A sessions to encourage interaction and make your audience feel valued and heard.

3. Use Relevant Hashtags Strategically

Hashtags are powerful tools for increasing your content's discoverability and reaching new audiences on Instagram. Research relevant hashtags within your niche and incorporate them strategically into your posts to expand your reach. Use a mix of broad and niche hashtags to attract different user groups and increase the likelihood of discovery. Monitor trending hashtags and participate in relevant conversations to capitalize on current trends and maximize your exposure.

4. Leverage Instagram Features and Tools

Take advantage of Instagram's features and tools to enhance your organic growth efforts. Use Instagram Stories, IGTV, and Reels to diversify your content and engage your audience in different formats. Utilize features like polls, quizzes, and countdowns to encourage interaction and increase engagement. Explore Instagram Insights to gain valuable data about your audience and the performance of your content, and use this data to refine your strategy and optimize your approach for better results.

5. Collaborate with Influencers and Partners

Collaborating with influencers and brand partners can help you tap into new audiences and accelerate your organic growth on Instagram.

Identify influencers and brands that align with your values and target audience, and explore collaboration opportunities such as sponsored posts, takeovers, or joint giveaways. Leveraging the reach and credibility of influencers and partners can expose your brand to new followers who are interested in your products or services and increase your visibility within your niche.

6. Encourage User-Generated Content

User-generated content (UGC) is a powerful way to foster community engagement and drive organic growth on Instagram. Encourage your followers to create and share content featuring your products or brand using a branded hashtag or tagging your account. Showcase user-generated content on your profile and stories to demonstrate social proof and encourage others to participate. By involving your audience in the content creation process, you can strengthen their connection to your brand and amplify your reach organically.

Organic growth on Instagram requires a strategic approach focused on creating compelling content, engaging authentically with your audience, and leveraging the platform's features and tools effectively. By consistently delivering high-quality content, engaging in genuine interactions, using relevant hashtags strategically, collaborating with influencers and partners, and encouraging user-generated content, you can attract and retain a loyal following and achieve sustainable growth on Instagram. Stay committed to building meaningful relationships with your audience and providing value through your content, and you'll see your organic reach and engagement continue to grow over time.

4.3 Engaging with Followers and Building Community

Engaging with your followers and building a sense of community on Instagram is essential for fostering loyalty, increasing brand advocacy, and driving organic growth. By actively engaging with your audience, you can strengthen relationships, encourage meaningful interactions, and create a supportive and engaged community around your brand. In this section, we will explore effective strategies for engaging with followers and building a thriving community on Instagram.

1. Respond to Comments and Messages Promptly

Promptly responding to comments and direct messages shows your followers that you value their input and care about their opinions. Take the time to acknowledge and respond to each comment individually, whether it's a question, feedback, or a simple expression of appreciation. Engage in genuine conversations with your followers, ask questions, and encourage further interaction to build rapport and strengthen relationships.

2. Like and Share User-Generated Content

Show appreciation for your followers' support and contributions by liking and sharing user-generated content (UGC) featuring your brand or products. When followers tag your account or use your branded hashtag, take the opportunity to showcase their content on your profile or stories. This not only acknowledges their efforts but also fosters a sense of community and encourages others to create and share content related to your brand.

3. Host Interactive Q&A Sessions and Polls

Engage your audience in interactive Q&A sessions and polls to encourage participation and gather valuable feedback. Use Instagram Stories to pose questions, solicit opinions, or invite followers to ask you anything about your brand or industry. Encourage participation by responding to questions and sharing the results of polls, and use the insights gained to tailor your content and offerings to better meet your audience's needs and preferences.

4. Foster User Engagement with Contests and Challenges

Organize contests, challenges, or giveaways to incentivize user engagement and foster a sense of community among your followers. Encourage followers to participate by submitting entries, sharing their experiences, or completing specific tasks related to your brand or products. Promote your contests across your social channels and collaborate with influencers or partners to amplify reach and increase participation. Contests and challenges not only drive engagement but also provide opportunities for user-generated content and brand advocacy.

5. Create and Share Behind-the-Scenes Content

Give your followers an exclusive behind-the-scenes look at your brand or business to humanize your brand and strengthen connections with your audience. Share glimpses of your workspace, production process, team members, or day-to-day operations to provide transparency and authenticity. Showcasing the people behind your brand and sharing personal stories helps humanize your brand and fosters a sense of trust and familiarity among your followers.

6. Encourage Community Engagement with Branded Hashtags

Create and promote branded hashtags that encourage your followers to share their experiences, stories, or content related to your brand. Include your branded hashtag in your bio, posts, and stories, and encourage followers to use it when sharing content featuring your products or brand. Regularly monitor and engage with posts using your branded hashtag, and showcase user-generated content on your profile to foster a sense of community and encourage further engagement.

Engaging with followers and building a sense of community on Instagram is crucial for fostering loyalty, driving organic growth, and creating brand advocates. By responding to comments and messages promptly, liking and sharing user-generated content, hosting interactive Q&A sessions and polls, organizing contests and challenges, sharing behind-the-scenes content, and encouraging community engagement with branded hashtags, you can create a supportive and engaged community around your brand. Invest time and effort in building meaningful relationships with your followers, and you'll see your community grow stronger and more loyal over time.

4.4 Leveraging Collaborations and Influencer Partnerships

Collaborating with influencers and brand partnerships is a powerful strategy for expanding your reach, increasing brand awareness, and driving engagement on Instagram. Influencers have established credibility and a dedicated following within your target audience, making them valuable partners for promoting your brand and products. In this section, we will explore effective strategies for leveraging collaborations and influencer partnerships on Instagram.

1. Identify Relevant Influencers and Partners

Start by identifying influencers and brands that align with your values, target audience, and marketing objectives. Look for influencers whose audience demographics, interests, and engagement align with your brand, and explore potential collaboration opportunities. Consider factors such as follower count, engagement rate, content quality, and brand affinity when evaluating potential partners.

2. Establish Clear Objectives and Expectations

Before reaching out to influencers or partners, define clear objectives and expectations for the collaboration. Determine what you hope to achieve, whether it's increasing brand awareness, driving website traffic, or generating sales. Communicate your goals, brand messaging, and any specific requirements or guidelines to ensure alignment and transparency throughout the partnership.

3. Reach Out with Personalized Pitches

When reaching out to influencers or brands for collaboration, personalize your pitches to demonstrate genuine interest and relevance. Tailor your outreach messages to each potential partner, highlighting why you believe they are a good fit for your brand and how the collaboration can benefit both parties. Be respectful of their time and preferences, and offer clear incentives or benefits for their participation.

4. Collaborate on Authentic Content Creation

Collaborate with influencers and partners to create authentic and engaging content that resonates with their audience and aligns with your brand values. Provide influencers with creative freedom to showcase your products or brand in a way that feels natural and authentic to their personal style and content niche. Encourage them to share their genuine experiences and opinions to build trust and credibility with their followers.

5. Amplify Reach with Cross-Promotion

Amplify the reach and impact of your collaborations by cross-promoting content across your respective platforms and networks. Share influencer-created content on your brand's Instagram profile, website, or other marketing channels to expose it to a wider audience. Encourage influencers to promote the collaboration on their social channels and engage with their followers to drive traffic and engagement back to your brand.

6. Measure and Evaluate Performance

Monitor the performance of your collaborations and influencer partnerships to assess their effectiveness and ROI. Track key metrics such as reach, engagement, website traffic, and sales attributed to the partnership to gauge its impact on your marketing objectives. Use this data to identify successful strategies, optimize future collaborations, and refine your influencer marketing approach for better results.

7. Cultivate Long-Term Relationships

Focus on building long-term relationships with influencers and brand partners based on mutual respect, trust, and collaboration. Invest in nurturing relationships beyond individual campaigns by staying in touch, providing ongoing support, and offering exclusive opportunities or incentives. Cultivating long-term partnerships fosters loyalty and advocacy among influencers and partners, resulting in more authentic and impactful collaborations over time.

By identifying relevant influencers and partners, establishing clear objectives and expectations, collaborating on authentic content creation, amplifying reach through cross-promotion, measuring performance, and cultivating long-term relationships, you can harness the power of influencer marketing to achieve your marketing goals and grow your brand on Instagram. Stay proactive, adaptable, and committed to building meaningful partnerships that benefit both your brand and your collaborators, and you'll see the positive impact of influencer marketing on your Instagram presence and business success.

Chapter 5: Instagram Advertising

Instagram advertising offers businesses a powerful platform to reach and engage with their target audience, drive traffic, and increase conversions. With a variety of ad formats and targeting options, advertisers can create highly targeted and impactful campaigns to achieve their marketing objectives. In this chapter, we will explore the fundamentals of Instagram advertising, including ad formats, targeting strategies, best practices, and tips for maximizing ROI.

1. Understanding Instagram Ad Formats

Instagram offers a range of ad formats to suit different campaign goals and creative preferences. Understanding each ad format and its unique features can help you choose the most effective option for your advertising objectives. Common Instagram ad formats include:

- **Photo Ads**: Single-image ads that appear in users' feeds, allowing advertisers to showcase their products or brands in a visually appealing way.
- **Video Ads**: Ads featuring videos up to 60 seconds in length that autoplay in users' feeds, offering a dynamic and engaging way to communicate your message.
- **Carousel Ads**: Multi-image or multi-video ads that allow advertisers to showcase multiple products or features within a single ad unit, enabling storytelling and product showcases.
- **Stories Ads**: Full-screen ads that appear between users' stories, offering a vertical, immersive advertising experience that captivates users' attention.

- **IGTV Ads**: Ads that appear before, during, or after IGTV videos, allowing advertisers to reach audiences engaging with long-form video content on Instagram.

2. Targeting Strategies for Instagram Ads

Effective targeting is key to maximizing the impact and relevance of your Instagram ads. Instagram offers robust targeting options that allow advertisers to reach specific audiences based on demographics, interests, behaviors, and more. Some targeting strategies to consider include:

- **Demographic Targeting**: Target ads based on factors such as age, gender, location, language, and education level to reach audiences that match your ideal customer profile.
- **Interest Targeting**: Target users based on their interests, hobbies, and behaviors, allowing you to reach audiences with specific interests or affinities related to your products or services.
- **Behavioral Targeting**: Target users based on their past behaviors, such as purchase history, app usage, or interactions with your brand or website, to reach audiences with a demonstrated interest or intent.
- **Lookalike Audiences**: Create lookalike audiences based on your existing customer data or website visitors to reach new users who share similar characteristics and behaviors with your current customers.

3. Best Practices for Instagram Advertising

To create effective Instagram ads that drive results, consider the following best practices:

- **Compelling Visuals**: Use high-quality images or videos that grab attention and showcase your products or brand in the best light.
- **Clear Call-to-Action (CTA)**: Include a clear and compelling call-to-action that encourages users to take the desired action, whether it's making a purchase, signing up for a newsletter, or visiting your website.
- **A/B Testing**: Experiment with different ad creative, copy, and targeting options to identify what resonates best with your audience and drives the highest performance.
- **Mobile Optimization**: Ensure your ads are optimized for mobile viewing, as the majority of Instagram users access the platform on mobile devices.
- **Ad Frequency**: Monitor ad frequency to avoid overexposure and ad fatigue among your audience, and adjust your ad delivery settings accordingly.
- **Ad Placement**: Consider testing different ad placements, such as feeds, stories, or explore, to determine which performs best for your campaign objectives.

4. Tips for Maximizing ROI

To maximize the return on investment (ROI) of your Instagram advertising campaigns, consider the following tips:

- **Set Clear Objectives**: Define specific goals and KPIs for your campaigns, such as impressions, clicks, conversions, or ROI, and track performance against these metrics.
- **Optimize for Conversions**: Use conversion tracking and optimization to focus your budget on users most likely to take the desired action, such as making a purchase or signing up for a trial.
- **Monitor Performance**: Regularly monitor and analyze the performance of your ads using Instagram Insights or third-party analytics tools, and make data-driven adjustments to optimize your campaigns.
- **Test and Iterate**: Continuously test different ad creative, targeting options, and campaign settings to identify what works best for your audience and refine your approach over time.
- **Budget Allocation**: Allocate your budget strategically across different ad formats, targeting options, and campaign objectives to maximize reach and effectiveness.

Instagram advertising offers businesses a powerful platform to reach and engage with their target audience, drive traffic, and increase conversions. By understanding the various ad formats, targeting options, best practices, and tips for maximizing ROI, advertisers can create impactful campaigns that achieve their marketing objectives and drive business results on Instagram. Whether you're looking to increase brand awareness, drive website traffic, or boost sales, Instagram advertising provides a flexible and effective solution for reaching your target audience and achieving your advertising goals.

5.1 Introduction to Instagram Ads

Instagram ads offer businesses a powerful way to reach and engage with their target audience on one of the world's most popular social media platforms. With over a billion active users worldwide, Instagram provides advertisers with a diverse and engaged audience that spans various demographics, interests, and locations. In this section, we will provide an overview of Instagram ads, including their benefits, key features, and the different types of ad formats available to advertisers.

Benefits of Instagram Ads

- **Massive Reach**: With over a billion monthly active users, Instagram offers advertisers a vast and diverse audience to connect with.
- **High Engagement**: Instagram boasts high levels of engagement, with users spending an average of 30 minutes per day on the platform, making it an ideal environment for driving interactions and conversions.
- **Visual Appeal**: As a visually-driven platform, Instagram allows advertisers to showcase their products or brands in a highly engaging and visually appealing way, leveraging the power of images and videos to captivate audiences.
- **Targeted Advertising**: Instagram offers robust targeting options that allow advertisers to reach specific audiences based on demographics, interests, behaviors, and more, ensuring that their ads are seen by the most relevant users.

Key Features of Instagram Ads

- **Sponsored Content**: Instagram ads appear seamlessly within users' feeds or stories, blending in with organic content to provide a native and non-disruptive advertising experience.
- **Call-to-Action Buttons**: Instagram ads include interactive call-to-action buttons that prompt users to take specific actions, such as visiting a website, downloading an app, or making a purchase.
- **Detailed Targeting Options**: Advertisers can target their ads based on a wide range of criteria, including age, gender, location, interests, behaviors, and more, allowing for precise audience segmentation and targeting.
- **Analytics and Insights**: Instagram provides advertisers with detailed analytics and insights into their ad performance, including metrics such as impressions, reach, engagement, clicks, and conversions, enabling them to measure the effectiveness of their campaigns and make data-driven decisions.

Types of Instagram Ad Formats

Instagram offers a variety of ad formats to suit different campaign goals and creative preferences. Some of the most common ad formats include:

- **Photo Ads**: Single-image ads that allow advertisers to showcase their products or brands in a visually compelling way.
- **Video Ads**: Ads featuring videos up to 60 seconds in length, offering a dynamic and engaging way to communicate your message.

- **Carousel Ads**: Multi-image or multi-video ads that allow advertisers to showcase multiple products or features within a single ad unit, enabling storytelling and product showcases.
- **Stories Ads**: Full-screen ads that appear between users' stories, providing an immersive and engaging advertising experience.
- **IGTV Ads**: Ads that appear before, during, or after IGTV videos, allowing advertisers to reach audiences engaging with long-form video content on Instagram.

Instagram ads offer businesses a powerful platform to reach and engage with their target audience, drive traffic, and increase conversions. With a variety of ad formats, targeting options, and interactive features, Instagram ads provide advertisers with the tools they need to create impactful campaigns that achieve their marketing objectives and drive business results. Whether you're looking to increase brand awareness, drive website traffic, or boost sales, Instagram ads offer a flexible and effective solution for reaching your target audience and achieving your advertising goals.

5.2 Setting Up Ad Campaigns and Targeting Options

Setting up ad campaigns on Instagram involves a series of steps to define your objectives, create compelling ad creatives, and target your desired audience effectively. Instagram provides advertisers with a range of targeting options to reach specific demographics, interests, behaviors, and more. In this section, we will explore the process of setting up ad campaigns on Instagram, including campaign objectives, ad formats, targeting options, and best practices for maximizing campaign effectiveness.

1. Define Your Campaign Objectives

The first step in setting up an ad campaign on Instagram is to define your campaign objectives. Consider what you want to achieve with your campaign, whether it's increasing brand awareness, driving website traffic, generating leads, or boosting sales. Your campaign objectives will influence your ad creative, targeting strategy, and measurement metrics, so it's essential to clearly define your goals from the outset.

2. Choose Your Ad Format and Creative

Next, choose the ad format and creative that best aligns with your campaign objectives and resonates with your target audience. Instagram offers a variety of ad formats, including photo ads, video ads, carousel ads, story ads, and IGTV ads. Select the ad format that best showcases your products or brand and captures users' attention. Create compelling ad creatives that tell a story, evoke emotion, and prompt users to take action.

3. Select Your Target Audience

Instagram provides advertisers with robust targeting options to reach specific audiences based on demographics, interests, behaviors, and more. Define your target audience based on factors such as age, gender, location, language, interests, hobbies, and purchase behavior. Use detailed targeting options to refine your audience further and ensure that your ads are seen by the most relevant users who are likely to engage with your content and take the desired action.

4. Set Your Budget and Schedule

Determine your budget and bidding strategy for your Instagram ad campaign. Decide whether you want to set a daily or lifetime budget and choose your bidding strategy based on your campaign objectives, whether it's maximizing reach, optimizing for conversions, or maximizing return on ad spend (ROAS). Set the duration and schedule for your campaign to control when your ads are shown and how often they appear to your target audience.

5. Measure and Optimize Performance

Once your ad campaign is live, monitor its performance closely using Instagram Insights or third-party analytics tools. Track key metrics such as impressions, reach, engagement, clicks, conversions, and return on investment (ROI) to evaluate the effectiveness of your campaign. Use this data to optimize your ad creative, targeting options, and bidding strategy for better results. Experiment with different variables, such as ad copy, imagery, audience segments, and bidding strategies, to identify what works best for your campaign objectives and audience.

Best Practices for Instagram Ad Campaigns

- **Start with Clear Objectives**: Define specific, measurable objectives for your ad campaign to guide your strategy and measurement efforts.

- **Create Compelling Ad Creatives**: Use high-quality images or videos and compelling ad copy to capture users' attention and encourage engagement.
- **Refine Your Target Audience**: Use detailed targeting options to reach the most relevant audience for your campaign objectives and refine your audience segments based on performance data.
- **Test and Iterate**: Continuously test different ad creatives, targeting options, and bidding strategies to identify what resonates best with your audience and drives the highest performance.
- **Monitor Performance Metrics**: Regularly monitor key performance metrics and adjust your campaign settings as needed to optimize performance and maximize ROI.

Setting up ad campaigns on Instagram involves careful planning, creative execution, and strategic targeting to achieve your campaign objectives and drive results. By defining clear objectives, choosing the right ad format and creative, selecting the appropriate target audience, setting your budget and schedule, and measuring and optimizing performance, you can create effective Instagram ad campaigns that reach and engage your target audience and drive meaningful business outcomes. Stay proactive, monitor performance closely, and iterate on your strategies to continuously improve your Instagram advertising efforts and achieve success on the platform.

5.3 Creating Effective Ad Content

Creating effective ad content is essential for capturing users' attention, driving engagement, and achieving your campaign objectives on Instagram. With visually-driven content and compelling messaging, advertisers can create ads that resonate with their target audience and prompt them to take action. In this section, we will explore best practices for creating effective ad content on Instagram, including tips for crafting compelling visuals, writing engaging ad copy, and incorporating calls to action.

1. Compelling Visuals

Visual content is king on Instagram, so it's crucial to create compelling visuals that grab users' attention and convey your message effectively. Use high-quality images or videos that showcase your products or brand in a visually appealing way. Consider the aesthetics of your feed and ensure that your ad creative aligns with your brand's visual identity and style. Experiment with different colors, compositions, and visual elements to create eye-catching and memorable ads that stand out in users' feeds.

2. Engaging Ad Copy

In addition to compelling visuals, engaging ad copy is essential for conveying your message and prompting users to take action. Write concise and persuasive ad copy that highlights the benefits of your products or services and encourages users to learn more or make a purchase. Use a clear and compelling call-to-action (CTA) that prompts users to take the desired action, whether it's visiting your website, making a purchase, or signing up for a newsletter. Tailor your messaging to resonate with your target audience and address their needs, pain points, and aspirations.

3. Authentic Storytelling

Authentic storytelling is key to connecting with users on Instagram and building trust and credibility with your audience. Use your ad content to tell a story that resonates with users on a personal level and showcases the value and benefits of your products or brand. Share behind-the-scenes glimpses of your brand or highlight real customer stories and testimonials to humanize your brand and foster a sense of authenticity. Authenticity builds trust and loyalty with your audience and encourages them to engage with your content and brand.

4. Incorporating User-Generated Content

User-generated content (UGC) is a powerful way to create authentic and relatable ad content that resonates with users. Incorporate UGC into your ad creative to showcase real-life experiences and testimonials from your customers. Encourage users to create and share content featuring your products or brand using a branded hashtag or tagging your account. By leveraging UGC, you can tap into the creativity and authenticity of your audience and build a stronger connection with your community.

5. Testing and Optimization

Once you've created your ad content, it's essential to test and optimize your creative to maximize its effectiveness. Experiment with different ad creatives, messaging tones, and visual elements to identify what resonates best with your target audience. Test variables such as ad copy, imagery, call-to-action buttons, and audience segments to determine which combinations drive the highest performance. Monitor key performance metrics such as engagement, click-through rate, and conversion rate, and use this data to optimize your ad creative for better results.

Creating effective ad content on Instagram requires a combination of compelling visuals, engaging ad copy, authentic storytelling, and strategic testing and optimization. By crafting visually appealing and emotionally resonant content, addressing the needs and aspirations of your target audience, and incorporating authentic storytelling and user-generated content, you can create ads that capture users' attention, drive engagement, and prompt them to take action. Continuously test and iterate on your ad creative to identify what resonates best with your audience and optimize your campaigns for maximum impact and ROI.

5.4 Analyzing Ad Performance and ROI

Analyzing ad performance and return on investment (ROI) is essential for evaluating the effectiveness of your Instagram advertising campaigns and making data-driven decisions to optimize future efforts. By monitoring key performance metrics and measuring the impact of your ads on business outcomes, you can identify areas for improvement, refine your strategies, and maximize the ROI of your advertising investment. In this section, we will explore best practices for analyzing ad performance and ROI on Instagram.

1. Monitor Key Performance Metrics

Start by monitoring key performance metrics to assess the effectiveness of your Instagram ads. Some essential metrics to track include:

- **Impressions**: The total number of times your ad was displayed to users.
- **Reach**: The number of unique users who saw your ad.
- **Engagement**: The total number of likes, comments, shares, and saves on your ad.
- **Click-Through Rate (CTR)**: The percentage of users who clicked on your ad after seeing it.
- **Conversion Rate**: The percentage of users who completed a desired action, such as making a purchase or signing up for a newsletter, after clicking on your ad.
- **Return on Ad Spend (ROAS)**: The ratio of revenue generated to the cost of advertising, calculated as revenue divided by ad spend.

2. Measure Impact on Business Outcomes

In addition to tracking engagement metrics, measure the impact of your Instagram ads on business outcomes such as website traffic, lead generation, and sales. Use tracking tools such as Facebook Pixel or conversion tracking tags to attribute conversions and revenue to specific ad campaigns. Analyze conversion data to understand which ads are driving the most valuable actions and generating the highest ROI for your business.

3. A/B Test Different Variables

Conduct A/B tests to experiment with different ad creative, messaging, targeting options, and bidding strategies to identify what resonates best with your audience and drives the highest performance. Test variables such as ad copy, imagery, call-to-action buttons, audience segments, and ad placements to determine which combinations result in the highest engagement and conversion rates. Use the insights gained from A/B testing to optimize your ad creative and targeting strategies for better results.

4. Optimize Based on Insights

Use the insights gained from analyzing ad performance to optimize your Instagram advertising campaigns for better results. Identify trends and patterns in your data, such as which ad formats, targeting options, or messaging tones perform best with your audience, and adjust your strategies accordingly. Allocate your budget to the most effective campaigns and ad sets, and reallocate resources away from underperforming campaigns to maximize ROI.

5. Continuously Iterate and Improve

Instagram advertising is an iterative process, so it's essential to continuously iterate and improve your campaigns based on performance data and insights. Regularly review your ad performance metrics, test new ideas and strategies, and refine your targeting, messaging, and creativity to optimize your campaigns for maximum impact and ROI. Stay informed about changes to the Instagram algorithm and advertising platform, and adapt your strategies accordingly to stay ahead of the curve.

Analyzing ad performance and ROI is critical for evaluating the effectiveness of your Instagram advertising campaigns and optimizing your strategies for better results. By monitoring key performance metrics, measuring the impact of your ads on business outcomes, conducting A/B tests, optimizing based on insights, and continuously iterating and improving your campaigns, you can maximize the ROI of your advertising investment and drive meaningful business results on Instagram. Stay proactive, data-driven, and adaptive in your approach, and you'll see the positive impact of Instagram advertising on your business growth and success.

Chapter 6: Engaging and Retaining Followers

Engaging and retaining followers on Instagram is essential for building a loyal and active community around your brand, fostering brand advocacy, and driving long-term success on the platform. By providing valuable content, fostering meaningful interactions, and building relationships with your audience, you can create a strong and engaged following that supports your brand and drives business outcomes. In this chapter, we will explore strategies for engaging and retaining followers on Instagram, including tips for creating compelling content, fostering community, and maintaining an active presence on the platform.

1. Providing Value-Driven Content

The foundation of engaging and retaining followers on Instagram is providing valuable content that resonates with your audience and meets their needs and interests. Create content that educates, entertains, inspires, or informs your followers, providing them with valuable insights, tips, or entertainment that enriches their experience on the platform. Consider the preferences and interests of your target audience when creating content and strive to deliver content that is relevant, timely, and meaningful to them.

2. Fostering Meaningful Interactions

Engage with your followers authentically and meaningfully to build relationships and foster a sense of community on Instagram. Respond to comments, messages, and mentions promptly, acknowledging and appreciating your followers' contributions and feedback. Initiate conversations, ask questions, and encourage user-generated content to foster engagement and dialogue with your audience. By actively engaging with your followers, you can strengthen relationships, build trust, and create a loyal and supportive community around your brand.

3. Building Relationships with Influencers and Partners

Collaborate with influencers and brand partners to leverage their influence and reach on Instagram and expand your brand's visibility and credibility. Partner with influencers who resonate with your target audience and share your brand values, collaborating on co-branded content, giveaways, or sponsored posts to reach new audiences and drive engagement. Build mutually beneficial relationships with influencers and partners based on trust, transparency, and shared goals, and leverage their influence to amplify your brand message and foster community engagement.

4. Encouraging User-Generated Content

Empower your followers to become brand advocates by encouraging user-generated content (UGC) and showcasing their contributions on your Instagram profile. Encourage users to create and share content featuring your products or brand by running contests, challenges, or campaigns that incentivize participation and creativity. Highlight UGC on your profile, stories, or feed to showcase your community's creativity and enthusiasm and encourage further engagement and participation from your followers.

5. Consistency and Authenticity

Maintain a consistent and authentic presence on Instagram by posting regularly and aligning your content with your brand values and identity. Develop a content strategy and posting schedule that resonates with your audience and reflects your brand's personality and voice. Be transparent, genuine, and relatable in your interactions with your followers, and share behind-the-scenes glimpses of your brand to humanize your content and build trust with your audience. Consistency and authenticity are key to building lasting relationships and retaining followers on Instagram.

Engaging and retaining followers on Instagram requires providing valuable content, fostering meaningful interactions, and building relationships with your audience and influencers. By creating content that resonates with your audience, engaging authentically with your followers, collaborating with influencers and partners, encouraging user-generated content, and maintaining consistency and authenticity in your brand's presence, you can build a loyal and engaged following that supports your brand and drives business outcomes on Instagram. Invest time and effort in building relationships and providing value to your followers, and you'll see your community grow stronger and more loyal over time.

6.1 Techniques for Increasing Engagement (Likes, Comments, Shares)

Increasing engagement on Instagram is essential for building a thriving community around your brand and driving meaningful interactions with your audience. By implementing effective techniques and strategies, you can encourage followers to like, comment, and share your content, amplifying your reach and fostering deeper connections with your audience. In this section, we will explore techniques for increasing engagement on Instagram, including tips for creating compelling content, fostering interaction, and encouraging participation from your followers.

1. Create Compelling Visuals

Start by creating visually appealing and attention-grabbing content that stands out in users' feeds. Use high-quality images or videos that showcase your products or brand in an aesthetically pleasing way. Experiment with different colors, compositions, and visual elements to create eye-catching content that captures users' attention and encourages them to engage with your posts.

2. Write Engaging Captions

Craft engaging captions that complement your visual content and encourage users to engage with your posts. Ask questions, spark curiosity, or share interesting stories or anecdotes to prompt users to comment and join the conversation. Use emojis, hashtags, and mentions strategically to add personality and context to your captions and make them more engaging and relatable to your audience.

3. Encourage Interaction

Encourage interaction with your content by inviting users to like, comment, or share your posts. Include clear and compelling calls-to-action (CTAs) in your captions or as overlays on your images or videos to prompt users to take specific actions. Encourage users to tag friends, share their thoughts or experiences, or participate in polls, quizzes, or challenges to foster engagement and dialogue with your audience.

4. Respond Promptly to Comments

Show appreciation for your followers' engagement by responding promptly and thoughtfully to comments on your posts. Acknowledge and thank users for their comments, answer any questions they may have, and engage in conversations to build rapport and strengthen relationships with your audience. By actively engaging with your followers, you demonstrate that you value their input and encourage further interaction and participation.

5. Host Giveaways and Contests

Host giveaways, contests, or challenges to incentivize engagement and reward your followers for their participation. Encourage users to like, comment, share, or tag friends to enter the contest or qualify for prizes, driving engagement and expanding your reach to new audiences. Be transparent and clear about the rules and guidelines of the contest, and ensure that the prizes are relevant and appealing to your target audience to maximize participation and engagement.

6. Share User-Generated Content

Empower your followers to become content creators by sharing user-generated content (UGC) on your Instagram profile. Highlight and showcase UGC featuring your products or brand to demonstrate social proof and encourage further engagement and participation from your followers. Tag and credit the original creators in your posts to acknowledge their contributions and foster a sense of community and collaboration with your audience.

Increasing engagement on Instagram requires a combination of compelling visuals, engaging captions, interaction prompts, responsive engagement, contests, and user-generated content. By implementing these techniques and strategies, you can encourage followers to like, comment, and share your content, fostering deeper connections with your audience and building a thriving community around your brand on Instagram. Experiment with different approaches, monitor your results and refine your strategies to maximize engagement and create meaningful interactions with your audience.

6.2 Hosting Contests and Giveaways

Hosting contests and giveaways on Instagram is a powerful strategy for increasing engagement, expanding your reach, and rewarding your followers for their loyalty and support. By offering enticing prizes and encouraging participation, you can generate excitement around your brand, attract new followers, and foster a sense of community and excitement among your audience. In this section, we will explore the steps for hosting successful contests and giveaways on Instagram, including planning, execution, and promotion strategies.

1. Define Your Goals and Objectives

Start by defining clear goals and objectives for your contest or giveaway. Consider what you want to achieve with your promotion, whether it's increasing brand awareness, driving engagement, growing your follower count, or promoting a new product or service. Your goals will guide your strategy and help you measure the success of your contest or giveaway.

2. Choose a Prize and Entry Method

Select a prize that is relevant and appealing to your target audience and aligns with your brand and objectives. The prize could be a product or service from your brand, a gift card, a special experience, or a collaboration with a partner or sponsor. Determine the entry method for your contest or giveaway, such as liking a post, commenting, tagging friends, sharing content, or submitting user-generated content. Choose entry methods that are easy to participate in and encourage engagement with your brand.

3. Set Clear Rules and Guidelines

Establish clear rules and guidelines for your contest or giveaway to ensure fairness and transparency. Clearly outline the eligibility criteria, entry requirements, entry period, prize details, winner selection process, and any additional terms and conditions. Communicate the rules and guidelines clearly and prominently in your contest or giveaway post and provide a link to the full terms and conditions for reference.

4. Create Compelling Content and Promotion

Create visually appealing and compelling content to promote your contest or giveaway on Instagram. Design eye-catching graphics, videos, or carousel posts that showcase the prize and communicate the entry instructions and rules. Use attention-grabbing captions, emojis, and hashtags to generate excitement and encourage participation from your followers. Promote your contest or giveaway across your Instagram profile, stories, and other social media channels to reach a wider audience and maximize participation.

5. Engage with Participants and Announce Winners

Engage with participants throughout your contest or giveaway by responding to comments, answering questions, and encouraging further engagement. Announce the winner(s) promptly and publicly on your Instagram profile, stories, or posts, and congratulate them on their win. Be transparent and fair in the winner selection process, and follow through on delivering the prize to the winner(s) promptly.

6. Measure Success and Learn from Feedback

After your contest or giveaway has ended, evaluate its success based on your pre-defined goals and objectives. Measure key metrics such as engagement, follower growth, website traffic, and conversions to assess the impact of your promotion. Solicit feedback from participants through surveys or direct messages to gather insights into their experience and preferences. Use this feedback to refine your future contest and giveaway strategies and improve the overall effectiveness of your promotions.

Hosting contests and giveaways on Instagram is an effective strategy for increasing engagement, expanding your reach, and rewarding your followers. By defining clear goals, choosing enticing prizes, setting clear rules, creating compelling content, promoting your promotion, engaging with participants, and measuring success, you can host successful contests and giveaways that drive meaningful results for your brand. Experiment with different contest formats and promotion strategies, and tailor your approach to resonate with your audience and achieve your objectives on Instagram.

6.3 Utilizing Instagram Stories and Live Features

Instagram Stories and Live features provide powerful tools for engaging with your audience in real time, fostering authenticity, and driving engagement on the platform. By leveraging these features creatively and strategically, you can create compelling content, connect with your audience on a deeper level, and build a stronger community around your brand. In this section, we will explore techniques for utilizing Instagram Stories and Live features effectively, including tips for creating engaging content, maximizing visibility, and fostering interaction with your audience.

1. Creating Engaging Stories and Content

Create engaging and visually compelling content for your Instagram Stories to capture users' attention and encourage them to engage with your brand. Use a variety of content formats, including photos, videos, boomerangs, and GIFs, to keep your Stories dynamic and interesting. Experiment with interactive features such as polls, quizzes, questions, and countdowns to encourage participation and feedback from your audience. Share behind-the-scenes glimpses of your brand, product demonstrations, tutorials, or sneak peeks to provide value and foster a sense of authenticity with your audience.

2. Going Live with Authentic and Interactive Broadcasts

Utilize Instagram Live to connect with your audience in real time and create authentic and interactive experiences. Host live Q&A sessions, interviews, product launches, demonstrations, or behind-the-scenes tours to engage with your audience and provide valuable insights or entertainment. Encourage viewers to ask questions, leave comments, and interact with you during the broadcast to foster a sense of community and participation. Be genuine, spontaneous, and transparent in your interactions, and showcase your brand's personality and values to connect with your audience on a deeper level.

3. Maximizing Visibility and Reach

Maximize the visibility and reach of your Instagram Stories and Live broadcasts by leveraging key features and strategies. Use relevant hashtags, location tags, and stickers to increase discoverability and reach a wider audience. Share your Stories at strategic times when your audience is most active to maximize engagement and visibility. Cross-promote your Stories and Live broadcasts on your other social media channels and in your Instagram feed to drive traffic and encourage participation from your followers.

4. Encouraging Interaction and Engagement

Encourage interaction and engagement with your Instagram Stories and Live broadcasts by inviting viewers to participate and interact with your content. Prompt viewers to ask questions, share their thoughts or experiences, or vote in polls and quizzes to foster engagement and dialogue. Respond to comments and questions in real-time during your Live broadcasts to make viewers feel heard and valued. Encourage viewers to share your Stories or invite friends to join your Live broadcasts to expand your reach and grow your audience organically.

5. Repurposing and Highlighting Content

Repurpose your Instagram Stories and Live broadcasts by saving them to your profile as Highlights, allowing viewers to revisit and discover your content even after it has expired. Organize your Highlights into thematic categories or topics to make it easy for users to find and explore relevant content. Highlight your best-performing Stories and most engaging Live broadcasts to showcase your brand's personality, values, and offerings and attract new followers to your profile.

By creating engaging Stories content, hosting authentic and interactive Live broadcasts, maximizing visibility and reach, encouraging interaction and engagement, and repurposing and highlighting your content, you can leverage these features effectively to build a stronger community around your brand and drive meaningful results on Instagram. Experiment with different content formats, interactive features, and engagement strategies to find what resonates best with your audience and achieves your objectives on the platform.

6.4 Responding to Comments and Direct Messages

Responding to comments and direct messages on Instagram is essential for building relationships, fostering engagement, and providing excellent customer service to your audience. By actively engaging with your followers and addressing their questions, feedback, and inquiries in a timely and thoughtful manner, you can strengthen connections with your audience and build trust and loyalty in your community. In this section, we will explore techniques for responding to comments and direct messages effectively, including tips for managing your inbox, providing personalized responses, and fostering meaningful interactions with your audience.

1. Monitor Your Inbox Regularly

Make it a priority to monitor your Instagram inbox regularly to stay on top of incoming comments and direct messages from your followers. Set aside dedicated time each day to review and respond to messages, or assign a team member to manage your inbox and ensure timely responses. Use Instagram's notifications and message filters to prioritize and organize incoming messages based on their importance and urgency, allowing you to focus on addressing the most pressing inquiries and feedback first.

2. Provide Timely and Personalized Responses

Respond to comments and direct messages promptly and personally to show your followers that you value their input and are attentive to their needs and concerns. Address users by name whenever possible and tailor your responses to their specific inquiries or comments to provide relevant and helpful information. Acknowledge and thank users for their comments, answer any questions they may have, and engage in meaningful conversations to build rapport and foster a sense of connection with your audience.

3. Be Transparent and Authentic

Be transparent and authentic in your interactions with your audience, and avoid canned or generic responses that feel impersonal or automated. Be honest and genuine in your responses, and admit when you don't have all the answers or when you make mistakes. Transparency builds trust and credibility with your audience and demonstrates that you are committed to providing honest and reliable information and support to your followers.

4. Use Instagram's Messaging Tools Effectively

Take advantage of Instagram's messaging tools and features to streamline your communication with your audience and provide better support and assistance. Use quick replies, saved replies, and automated responses to handle common inquiries and frequently asked questions efficiently. Leverage Instagram's tagging and mention features to notify relevant team members or departments and collaborate on providing comprehensive and timely responses to users' inquiries and feedback.

5. Foster Meaningful Interactions and Relationships

Go beyond simply answering questions or addressing complaints, and strive to foster meaningful interactions and relationships with your audience. Initiate conversations, ask questions, and encourage users to share their thoughts, experiences, and feedback with you. Engage with users authentically and authentically, and take the time to listen to their concerns, ideas, and suggestions. By fostering open and respectful dialogue with your audience, you can build stronger relationships and create a loyal and engaged community around your brand on Instagram.

Responding to comments and direct messages on Instagram is a crucial aspect of engaging with your audience, providing excellent customer service, and building relationships with your followers. By monitoring your inbox regularly, providing timely and personalized responses, being transparent and authentic, using Instagram's messaging tools effectively, and fostering meaningful interactions and relationships with your audience, you can strengthen connections with your community and create a positive and supportive environment for your followers on Instagram. Prioritize responsiveness and engagement, and make it a priority to listen to and address the needs and concerns of your audience to build trust and loyalty with your community over time.

Chapter 7: Advanced Instagram Marketing Strategies

In Chapter 7, we will delve into advanced Instagram marketing strategies that go beyond the basics and help you elevate your brand's presence, engagement, and impact on the platform. These strategies are designed to help you stand out in a crowded digital landscape, reach new audiences, and drive meaningful business results. From leveraging emerging trends to optimizing your advertising campaigns, this chapter will equip you with the knowledge and techniques you need to take your Instagram marketing efforts to the next level.

1. Embracing Emerging Trends

Stay ahead of the curve by embracing emerging trends and features on Instagram. From new content formats like Reels and Guides to evolving engagement tactics such as interactive stickers and shopping bags, there are always new opportunities to explore and experiment with on the platform. Keep a close eye on industry trends, monitor changes to the Instagram algorithm, and adapt your strategy accordingly to leverage emerging trends effectively and stay relevant to your audience.

2. Harnessing the Power of User-Generated Content (UGC)

User-generated content (UGC) is a valuable asset for brands on Instagram, providing authentic social proof and driving engagement and trust with your audience. Develop a UGC strategy that encourages your followers to create and share content featuring your products or brand. Host UGC contests or challenges, showcase user-generated content on your profile and engage with your community to foster a culture of co-creation and collaboration. By harnessing the power of UGC, you can amplify your brand's reach and credibility on Instagram.

3. Leveraging Influencer Partnerships

Collaborate with influencers and brand ambassadors to amplify your brand's message and reach new audiences on Instagram. Partner with influencers who align with your brand values and have a genuine connection with their followers. Develop authentic and mutually beneficial partnerships that allow influencers to create engaging content featuring your products or brand and share it with their audience. Track the performance of influencer campaigns and measure their impact on your brand awareness, engagement, and conversions to optimize your influencer marketing strategy effectively.

4. Implementing Advanced Advertising Strategies

Take your Instagram advertising campaigns to the next level with advanced targeting, optimization, and creative strategies. Experiment with custom audience targeting, lookalike audience modeling, and retargeting tactics to reach specific segments of your audience with personalized messaging and offers. Optimize your ad creative and copy based on performance data and A/B testing results to maximize engagement and conversions. Explore advanced ad formats such as dynamic ads, collection ads, and augmented reality (AR) experiences to captivate and convert your audience effectively.

5. Measuring and Analyzing Performance

Measure the success of your Instagram marketing efforts by tracking key performance metrics and analyzing the impact of your campaigns on your business outcomes. Use Instagram Insights, third-party analytics tools, and custom tracking parameters to monitor metrics such as reach, engagement, click-through rate (CTR), conversion rate, and return on investment (ROI). Analyze trends and patterns in your data, identify areas for improvement, and iterate on your strategy to optimize performance and achieve your marketing goals effectively.

Advanced Instagram marketing strategies offer powerful opportunities for brands to elevate their presence, engagement, and impact on the platform. By embracing emerging trends, harnessing the power of user-generated content, leveraging influencer partnerships, implementing advanced advertising strategies, and measuring and analyzing performance, you can unlock new opportunities for growth and success on Instagram. Experiment with these advanced strategies, stay agile and adaptive in your approach and continuously iterate and optimize your efforts to achieve meaningful results and drive business outcomes on the platform.

7.1 Utilizing Instagram Shopping and Product Tags

Instagram Shopping and Product Tags are powerful features that allow brands to showcase their products directly within their Instagram posts and stories, making it easier for users to discover, browse, and purchase products without leaving the app. By leveraging these features effectively, brands can drive sales, increase product visibility, and create seamless shopping experiences for their audience. In this section, we will explore techniques for utilizing Instagram Shopping and Product

Tags to maximize your brand's presence and sales potential on the platform.

1. Setting Up Your Instagram Shop

Start by setting up your Instagram Shop to enable Shopping and Product Tags on your account. Ensure that your account meets the eligibility criteria for Instagram Shopping, which includes having a business account, complying with Instagram's merchant agreement and commerce policies, and selling physical goods that comply with Instagram's commerce policies. Connect your Instagram account to your Facebook Business Page, set up a product catalog using Facebook Commerce Manager, and submit your account for review to get approval for Instagram Shopping.

2. Tagging Products in Your Posts and Stories

Once your Instagram Shop is set up and approved, you can start tagging products in your posts and stories. Create high-quality content featuring your products, such as product photos, videos, or lifestyle shots, and add product tags to highlight specific items featured in your content. When users tap on a product tag, they will see product details, including the name, price, and a direct link to purchase the product on your website. Tag multiple products in a single post or story to showcase your product range and provide users with more options to explore and shop.

3. Creating Shoppable Posts and Stories

Design shoppable posts and stories that encourage users to engage with your content and explore your products further. Use compelling visuals, engaging captions, and clear calls-to-action (CTAs) to prompt users to tap on product tags and learn more about the featured products. Incorporate interactive features such as polls, quizzes, or countdown stickers to increase engagement and encourage users to interact with your shoppable content. Experiment with different content formats and storytelling techniques to keep your audience engaged and motivated to shop.

4. Optimizing Product Descriptions and Details

Optimize your product descriptions and details to provide users with valuable information and encourage them to make a purchase. Write concise and informative product descriptions that highlight the key features, benefits, and unique selling points of each product. Use high-quality images and videos that showcase your products from different angles and provide users with a clear view of what they can expect. Include relevant hashtags, mentions, and product tags in your captions to increase discoverability and reach more potential customers on Instagram.

5. Tracking Performance and Iterating on Strategies

Monitor the performance of your shoppable posts and stories using Instagram Insights and other analytics tools to track metrics such as engagement, click-through rate (CTR), and conversion rate. Analyze which products are generating the most interest and sales, and identify trends and patterns in user behavior to optimize your product tagging and content strategy accordingly. Experiment with different product placements, content formats, and promotional tactics to improve performance and drive more sales through Instagram Shopping.

Instagram Shopping and Product Tags offer brands a powerful way to showcase their products and drive sales directly on the platform. By setting up your Instagram Shop, tagging products in your posts and stories, creating shoppable content, optimizing product descriptions and details, and tracking performance to iterate on your strategies, you can maximize the effectiveness of Instagram Shopping and unlock new opportunities for growth and success on the platform. Stay agile and adaptive in your approach, and continuously experiment with new techniques and features to drive more sales and create seamless shopping experiences for your audience on Instagram.

7.2 Exploring IGTV and Instagram Reels for Brand Building

IGTV and Instagram Reels are powerful video features on Instagram that offer brands unique opportunities to showcase their personality, creativity, and expertise, and connect with their audience in engaging and entertaining ways. By leveraging these features effectively, brands can increase their visibility, engagement, and brand awareness on the platform, and create memorable and shareable content that resonates with their audience. In this section, we will explore techniques for utilizing IGTV and Instagram Reels for brand building, including tips for content creation, promotion, and engagement.

1. Creating Compelling Video Content

Start by creating compelling and engaging video content that captures your brand's personality and resonates with your audience. Experiment with different content formats, such as tutorials, behind-the-scenes footage, product demonstrations, interviews, or storytelling, to keep your audience entertained and interested. Keep your videos concise and focused, and aim to deliver value or entertainment to your viewers within a short timeframe to maximize engagement and retention.

2. Showcasing Your Brand Story and Values

Use IGTV and Instagram Reels as platforms to showcase your brand's story, values, and mission in a visually compelling and authentic way. Share stories about your brand's journey, highlights from your company culture, or insights into your product development process to humanize your brand and build emotional connections with your audience. Align your content with your brand's values and messaging, and communicate your unique selling propositions effectively to differentiate yourself from competitors and resonate with your target audience.

3. Engaging Your Audience with Interactive Content

Engage your audience with interactive and immersive content experiences on IGTV and Instagram Reels. Use interactive features such as polls, quizzes, questions, and challenges to encourage participation and feedback from your viewers. Prompt viewers to interact with your content by asking questions, soliciting opinions, or inviting them to share their own experiences or stories related to your brand. Foster a sense of community and collaboration with your audience by acknowledging and responding to their comments and contributions.

4. Promoting Your Videos across Multiple Channels

Promote your IGTV and Instagram Reel videos across multiple channels to maximize visibility and reach. Share previews or highlights of your videos in your Instagram feed or stories to tease viewers and encourage them to watch the full content on IGTV or Instagram Reels. Cross-promote your videos on other social media platforms, your website, email newsletters, and other marketing channels to reach a wider audience and drive traffic to your Instagram profile. Collaborate with influencers, partners, or industry experts to amplify your reach and leverage your audience to increase exposure for your videos.

5. Analyzing Performance and Iterating on Strategies

Monitor the performance of your IGTV and Instagram Reels videos using Instagram Insights and other analytics tools to track metrics such as views, engagement, watch time, and follower growth. Analyze which types of content resonate most with your audience and drive the highest engagement and conversion rates. Experiment with different video formats, topics, lengths, and posting times to optimize your content strategy and improve performance over time. Use viewer feedback and comments to gain insights into your audience's preferences and interests and tailor your content to meet their needs effectively.

IGTV and Instagram Reels offer brands powerful opportunities to showcase their creativity, personality, and expertise and connect with their audience in meaningful and engaging ways. By creating compelling video content, showcasing your brand story and values, engaging your audience with interactive content, promoting your videos across multiple channels, and analyzing performance to iterate on your strategies, you can leverage IGTV and Instagram Reels effectively to build brand awareness, engagement, and loyalty on Instagram. Experiment with different techniques and content formats, and stay agile and adaptive in your approach to create memorable and impactful video content that resonates with your audience and drives business results for your brand on the platform.

7.3 Leveraging User-Generated Content

User-generated content (UGC) is a valuable asset for brands on Instagram, providing authentic social proof and driving engagement and trust with your audience. By leveraging UGC effectively, brands can amplify their reach, build credibility, and foster a sense of community and connection with their audience. In this section, we will explore techniques for leveraging user-generated content to enhance your brand's presence and impact on Instagram.

1. Encouraging User-Generated Content

Start by actively encouraging your audience to create and share content featuring your products or brand. Host UGC contests, challenges, or campaigns that incentivize participation and creativity from your followers. Create branded hashtags or tags that users can use to tag their content and make it discoverable to your brand. Share user-generated content on your Instagram profile, stories, or feed to showcase your community's creativity and enthusiasm and encourage further engagement and participation from your followers.

2. Showcasing User-Generated Content

Highlight and showcase user-generated content on your Instagram profile to demonstrate social proof and authenticity to your audience. Create dedicated highlights or albums featuring user-generated content to showcase the diversity and creativity of your community. Tag and credit the original creators in your posts to acknowledge their contributions and foster a sense of recognition and appreciation. Use user-generated content to complement your brand's content strategy and provide a fresh and authentic perspective to your audience.

3. Engaging with User-Generated Content

Engage with user-generated content authentically and meaningfully to build relationships and foster community on Instagram. Like, comment, and share user-generated content to show appreciation for your followers' contributions and encourage further participation and engagement. Respond to comments and messages from users who share content featuring your brand, and thank them for their support and advocacy. By actively engaging with user-generated content, you demonstrate that you value your community and appreciate their contributions to your brand.

4. Incorporating User-Generated Content into Marketing Campaigns

Integrate user-generated content into your marketing campaigns and initiatives to enhance their effectiveness and impact. Feature user-generated content in your advertising campaigns, website, email newsletters, and other marketing channels to showcase real-life testimonials and experiences from your customers. Use user-generated content to illustrate the benefits and value of your products or brand and inspire trust and confidence in your audience. By incorporating user-generated content into your marketing efforts, you can leverage the authenticity and credibility of your community to drive engagement and conversions effectively.

5. Monitoring and Measuring Performance

Monitor the performance of user-generated content using Instagram Insights and other analytics tools to track metrics such as engagement, reach, and conversions. Analyze which types of user-generated content resonate most with your audience and drive the highest levels of engagement and conversion rates. Use this data to inform your content strategy and identify opportunities for optimization and improvement. Measure the impact of user-generated content on your brand awareness, engagement, and sales to justify the investment in UGC initiatives and demonstrate their value to your organization.

Leveraging user-generated content is a powerful strategy for enhancing your brand's presence and impact on Instagram. By actively encouraging, showcasing, engaging with, incorporating, and measuring user-generated content, you can harness the authenticity and creativity of your community to drive engagement, build trust, and foster loyalty with your audience. Embrace UGC as a valuable asset in your Instagram marketing strategy, and empower your community to become brand advocates and ambassadors who contribute to your brand's success and growth on the platform.

7.4 Analyzing Competitor Strategies

Analyzing competitor strategies on Instagram is essential for staying informed about industry trends, identifying gaps in the market, and benchmarking your brand's performance against competitors. By understanding what strategies and tactics your competitors are employing on the platform, you can gain valuable insights into their strengths and weaknesses and identify opportunities for differentiation and improvement for your brand. In this section, we will explore techniques for analyzing competitor strategies on Instagram effectively.

1. Identify Your Competitors

Start by identifying your main competitors on Instagram within your industry or niche. Research brands that offer similar products or services to yours and have a presence on Instagram. Look for competitors with a similar target audience, market positioning, and level of engagement on the platform. Make a list of your competitors and prioritize those that are most relevant and influential within your industry.

2. Analyze Their Content Strategy

Study your competitors' content strategy on Instagram to understand the types of content they are creating and sharing with their audience. Analyze the frequency, format, and quality of their posts, as well as the themes, topics, and messaging they are using in their captions and visuals. Pay attention to the types of engagement their posts are receiving, such as likes, comments, and shares, and identify patterns or trends in their content strategy that contribute to their success on the platform.

3. Assess Their Engagement Tactics

Evaluate how your competitors are engaging with their audience on Instagram and fostering interaction and dialogue. Look at how they respond to comments, messages, and mentions from their followers, and analyze the tone, style, and frequency of their interactions. Pay attention to any engagement tactics or strategies they are using, such as hosting giveaways, running contests, or collaborating with influencers, and assess their effectiveness in driving engagement and building relationships with their audience.

4. Review Their Follower Growth Strategies

Examine how your competitors are growing their follower base on Instagram and attracting new audiences to their profiles. Look at the tactics and techniques they are using to promote their Instagram accounts, such as cross-promotion on other social media channels, influencer partnerships, or advertising campaigns. Analyze the quality of their follower growth, as well as the rate of growth over time, to assess the effectiveness of their follower acquisition strategies and identify opportunities for improvement for your brand.

5. Monitor Their Performance Metrics

Track and monitor the performance metrics of your competitors' Instagram profiles using Instagram Insights and other analytics tools. Pay attention to key metrics such as follower count, engagement rate, reach, impressions, and profile visits to gauge their overall performance and effectiveness on the platform. Compare your brand's performance metrics to those of your competitors to identify areas where you excel and areas where you may need to improve to remain competitive in the market.

6. Benchmark Your Brand against Competitors

Benchmark your brand's performance against your competitors to understand where you stand with your industry peers. Compare your content strategy, engagement tactics, follower growth strategies, and performance metrics to those of your competitors to identify strengths, weaknesses, opportunities, and threats for your brand. Use this information to refine your Instagram marketing strategy, differentiate your brand from competitors, and capitalize on opportunities to gain a competitive advantage on the platform.

Analyzing competitor strategies on Instagram is an important aspect of developing a successful Instagram marketing strategy for your brand. By identifying your competitors, analyzing their content strategy, assessing their engagement tactics, reviewing their follower growth strategies, monitoring their performance metrics, and benchmarking your brand against competitors, you can gain valuable insights into the competitive landscape and identify opportunities for improvement and differentiation for your brand on the platform. Stay informed about industry trends and best practices, and continuously iterate and optimize your Instagram marketing strategy to stay ahead of the competition and achieve your business goals effectively.

Chapter 8: Measuring Success and Adapting Your Strategy

In Chapter 8, we will explore the crucial process of measuring the success of your Instagram marketing efforts and adapting your strategy based on key insights and performance metrics. By effectively tracking and analyzing your performance on the platform, you can identify what's working well, what needs improvement, and where to focus your efforts to achieve your business goals. In this chapter, we will delve into techniques for measuring success on Instagram, including key performance indicators (KPIs) to track, tools for analytics and reporting, and strategies for optimizing your Instagram marketing strategy based on data-driven insights.

1. Defining Key Performance Indicators (KPIs)

Start by defining key performance indicators (KPIs) that align with your business objectives and goals on Instagram. These may include metrics such as follower growth, engagement rate, reach, impressions, click-through rate (CTR), conversion rate, and return on investment (ROI). By identifying the metrics that matter most to your business, you can track progress toward your goals and measure the success of your Instagram marketing efforts effectively.

2. Using Analytics Tools for Tracking and Reporting

Utilize analytics tools and platforms such as Instagram Insights, third-party analytics tools, and social media management software to track and report on your performance metrics. These tools provide valuable data and insights into your audience demographics, content performance, engagement patterns, and follower behavior, allowing you to gain a deeper understanding of your audience and optimize your content strategy accordingly.

3. Analyzing Performance Metrics and Trends

Regularly analyze your performance metrics and trends to identify patterns, opportunities, and areas for improvement. Look for trends in your audience engagement, content performance, and follower growth over time, and identify which types of content resonate most with your audience and drive the highest levels of engagement and conversion rates. Use this data to inform your content strategy, optimize your posting schedule, and refine your targeting and messaging to better meet the needs and preferences of your audience.

4. Experimenting with A/B Testing and Optimization

Experiment with A/B testing and optimization techniques to refine your Instagram marketing strategy and improve performance over time. Test different variables such as content formats, captions, hashtags, posting times, and ad creativity to identify what resonates best with your audience and drives the desired outcomes. Continuously iterate and refine your approach based on the results of your experiments, and incorporate learnings into future campaigns and initiatives to maximize effectiveness and ROI.

5. Adapting Your Strategy Based on Insights

Adapt your Instagram marketing strategy based on insights and learnings gathered from your performance metrics and analytics. Be flexible and agile in your approach, and be willing to pivot and adjust your strategy as needed to capitalize on opportunities and address challenges. Monitor industry trends, competitor activities, and changes to the Instagram algorithm, and adapt your strategy accordingly to stay ahead of the curve and maintain a competitive edge on the platform.

Measuring success and adapting your strategy based on insights is essential for achieving your business goals and driving meaningful results on Instagram. By defining key performance indicators (KPIs), using analytics tools for tracking and reporting, analyzing performance metrics and trends, experimenting with A/B testing and optimization, and adapting your strategy based on insights, you can optimize your Instagram marketing efforts and maximize your impact on the platform. Stay data-driven and results-oriented in your approach, and continuously iterate and refine your strategy to achieve long-term success and growth on Instagram.

8.1 Tools for Analyzing Performance Metrics

Analyzing performance metrics is crucial for understanding the effectiveness of your Instagram marketing efforts and making informed decisions to optimize your strategy. Fortunately, there are various tools available to help you track and analyze key metrics and gain valuable insights into your audience, content performance, and overall Instagram presence. In this section, we will explore some of the top tools for analyzing performance metrics on Instagram.

1. Instagram Insights

Instagram Insights is a built-in analytics tool provided by Instagram that offers valuable data and insights into your account's performance. With Instagram Insights, you can track metrics such as impressions, reach, engagement, follower demographics, and content interactions. Accessible directly from your Instagram business profile, Insights provides a comprehensive overview of your account's performance and allows you to monitor trends and identify opportunities for improvement.

2. Third-Party Analytics Tools

There are many third-party analytics tools available that offer advanced features and capabilities for tracking and analyzing Instagram performance metrics. Tools such as Hootsuite, Sprout Social, Buffer, and Later provide robust analytics dashboards that allow you to track key metrics, measure the effectiveness of your campaigns, and generate detailed reports on your Instagram performance. These tools often offer additional features such as scheduling, content planning, and audience segmentation, making them valuable resources for managing your Instagram presence.

3. Google Analytics

While Google Analytics primarily focuses on website traffic and conversions, it can also be used to track and analyze traffic from Instagram to your website. By setting up UTM parameters and tracking links in your Instagram bio or posts, you can measure the traffic, engagement, and conversion metrics generated from your Instagram marketing efforts. Google Analytics provides insights into user behavior, referral sources, and conversion paths, allowing you to assess the impact of your Instagram campaigns on your website's performance.

4. Social Media Management Platforms

Social media management platforms such as Agorapulse, Socialbakers, and Falcon.io offer comprehensive analytics features specifically designed for managing and analyzing performance across multiple social media channels, including Instagram. These platforms provide advanced reporting capabilities, customizable dashboards, and benchmarking tools that allow you to compare your performance against competitors and industry benchmarks. Additionally, they offer workflow automation, collaboration tools, and integration with other marketing platforms, making them valuable resources for managing and optimizing your Instagram marketing strategy.

5. Instagram Analytics Apps

There are also various mobile apps available that offer insights and analytics for Instagram performance on the go. Apps such as Iconosquare, Social Blade, and Followers Insight provide real-time metrics, follower insights, and engagement analytics directly from your mobile device. These apps offer convenient access to key performance metrics and allow you to monitor your Instagram account's performance and engagement levels anytime, anywhere.

Analyzing performance metrics is essential for optimizing your Instagram marketing strategy and achieving your business goals on the platform. By leveraging tools such as Instagram Insights, third-party analytics platforms, Google Analytics, social media management platforms, and Instagram analytics apps, you can gain valuable insights into your audience, content performance, and overall Instagram presence. Use these tools to track key metrics, measure the effectiveness of your campaigns, and make data-driven decisions to drive engagement, grow your following, and achieve success on Instagram.

8.2 Adjusting Your Strategy Based on Data

Adjusting your Instagram marketing strategy based on data-driven insights is essential for optimizing performance and achieving your business objectives on the platform. By analyzing key metrics and trends, you can identify what's working well and what needs improvement, and make informed decisions to refine your approach and maximize results. In this section, we will explore how to adjust your strategy based on data effectively.

1. Review Performance Metrics Regularly

Regularly review your performance metrics and analytics data to gain insights into your Instagram marketing efforts. Track metrics such as engagement rate, follower growth, reach, impressions, click-through rate (CTR), and conversion rate to understand how your content and campaigns are performing. Identify trends, patterns, and areas of opportunity or concern, and use this information to inform your strategy adjustments.

2. Identify Successful Tactics and Content

Identify successful tactics and content that are driving the highest levels of engagement, reach, and conversions on Instagram. Analyze which types of posts, content formats, captions, hashtags, and posting times resonate most with your audience and generate the best results. Double down on these successful tactics and content strategies, and incorporate them into your future content planning and campaign execution to amplify their impact.

3. Address Underperforming Areas

Address underperforming areas of your Instagram strategy by identifying areas where engagement, reach, or conversion rates are below expectations. Analyze the factors contributing to underperformance, such as content quality, relevance, timing, or targeting, and brainstorm strategies to improve performance in these areas. Experiment with different approaches, content formats, or messaging to see what resonates best with your audience and drives better results.

4. Test and Iterate

Test and iterate on your Instagram marketing strategy to refine your approach and optimize performance over time. Experiment with A/B testing to compare different variables, such as content formats, captions, hashtags, or posting times, and measure the impact on key metrics. Use insights from these tests to make data-driven decisions about which strategies to prioritize and which to refine or discard. Continuously iterate and evolve your strategy based on performance data and audience feedback to stay agile and adaptive in your approach.

5. Stay Flexible and Adaptive

Stay flexible and adaptive in your approach to adjusting your Instagram marketing strategy based on data. Be open to new ideas, trends, and opportunities that emerge from your analysis, and be willing to pivot or adjust your strategy as needed to capitalize on them. Monitor industry trends, competitor activities, and changes to the Instagram algorithm, and adapt your strategy accordingly to stay ahead of the curve and maintain a competitive edge on the platform.

Adjusting your Instagram marketing strategy based on data-driven insights is essential for maximizing results and achieving your business goals on the platform. By regularly reviewing performance metrics, identifying successful tactics and content, addressing underperforming areas, testing and iterating on your strategy, and staying flexible and adaptive in your approach, you can optimize your Instagram marketing efforts and drive engagement, growth, and conversions effectively. Use data to inform your decisions, and continuously refine and evolve your strategy to stay aligned with your audience's preferences and behaviors and achieve long-term success on Instagram.

8.3 Staying Updated with Instagram's Evolving Features

Staying updated with Instagram's evolving features is essential for maintaining a competitive edge and maximizing your success on the platform. As Instagram continues to introduce new tools, features, and updates, staying informed and adapting your strategy accordingly can help you leverage the latest capabilities to engage your audience, drive growth, and achieve your business objectives. In this section, we will explore strategies for staying updated with Instagram's evolving features effectively.

1. Follow Instagram's Official Channels

Stay informed about Instagram's latest updates and announcements by following Instagram's official channels on social media platforms such as Instagram, Twitter, and Facebook. Instagram often shares news, updates, and tips through its official accounts and blog posts, providing valuable insights into new features, changes to the algorithm, and best practices for using the platform effectively. Turn on notifications for these channels to receive real-time updates and stay ahead of the curve.

2. Join Instagram Community Groups and Forums

Join Instagram community groups and forums where marketers, businesses, and influencers gather to discuss trends, strategies, and updates related to the platform. Platforms such as Facebook Groups, LinkedIn Groups, and Reddit communities offer valuable opportunities to connect with peers, share insights, and stay updated on the latest Instagram news and developments. Participate in discussions, ask questions, and share your own experiences to learn from others and stay informed about industry trends.

3. Attend Instagram Webinars and Workshops

Attend webinars, workshops, and virtual events hosted by Instagram or industry experts to gain insights into the latest features, best practices, and strategies for success on the platform. Instagram often hosts educational events and training sessions for businesses and marketers, covering topics such as content creation, advertising, analytics, and community management. Participate in these events to learn from Instagram experts, ask questions, and stay updated on the latest trends and innovations.

4. Experiment with Beta Features and Test Builds

Keep an eye out for beta features and test builds that Instagram may roll out to select users for feedback and testing purposes. Participate in beta programs or sign up for early access to new features to get hands-on experience with cutting-edge tools and capabilities before they are widely available to the public. Experimenting with beta features allows you to gain a competitive advantage and explore innovative ways to engage your audience and differentiate your brand on the platform.

5. Follow Industry Thought Leaders and Influencers

Follow industry thought leaders, influencers, and experts who specialize in Instagram marketing and stay updated on the latest trends, strategies, and features shaping the platform. Subscribe to their newsletters, blogs, podcasts, and social media channels to receive insights, tips, and updates directly from those at the forefront of the industry. Engage with their content, participate in discussions, and leverage their expertise to stay informed and inspired in your own Instagram marketing efforts.

Staying updated with Instagram's evolving features is essential for maximizing your success and staying ahead of the competition on the platform. By following Instagram's official channels, joining community groups and forums, attending webinars and workshops, experimenting with beta features, and following industry thought leaders and influencers, you can stay informed about the latest trends, tools, and best practices for success on Instagram. Embrace a culture of continuous learning and experimentation, and adapt your strategy accordingly to leverage the latest features and innovations to engage your audience, drive growth, and achieve your business goals effectively on Instagram.

8.4 Case Studies of Successful Instagram Marketing Campaigns

Examining case studies of successful Instagram marketing campaigns provides valuable insights into effective strategies, tactics, and best practices for achieving success on the platform. By learning from real-world examples of brands that have excelled on Instagram, marketers can gain inspiration and ideas for their campaigns and initiatives. In this section, we will explore case studies of successful Instagram marketing campaigns across various industries.

1. Nike: #JustDoIt Campaign

Nike's #JustDoIt campaign is one of the most iconic and successful marketing campaigns in recent history, and Instagram played a crucial role in its success. By leveraging compelling visuals, inspiring storytelling, and user-generated content, Nike engaged its audience and built a community around the ethos of determination, athleticism, and empowerment. The campaign featured a diverse range of athletes, influencers, and everyday individuals sharing their stories of overcoming challenges and achieving greatness, resonating with Nike's target audience and driving engagement, brand affinity, and sales.

2. Glossier: #GlossierPink Campaign

Beauty brand Glossier is known for its minimalist aesthetic and strong Instagram presence, and its #GlossierPink campaign is a prime example of its success on the platform. By creating a dedicated hashtag and encouraging users to share photos of their favorite Glossier products featuring the signature pink packaging, Glossier fostered a sense of community and generated user-generated content that showcased the brand's products in real-life settings. The campaign generated millions of user-generated posts and helped Glossier build brand awareness, drive sales, and establish itself as a leader in the beauty industry on Instagram.

3. Airbnb: #LiveThere Campaign

Airbnb's #LiveThere campaign aimed to redefine travel and encourage users to experience destinations like locals rather than tourists. Through captivating visuals, immersive storytelling, and user-generated content, Airbnb showcased unique accommodations and experiences around the world, inspiring travelers to explore new destinations and create meaningful connections with local communities. The campaign generated widespread engagement and user participation, driving brand affinity, customer loyalty, and bookings for Airbnb properties.

4. National Geographic: #NatGeoTravel Photo Contest

National Geographic's #NatGeoTravel Photo Contest is an annual campaign that celebrates the beauty and diversity of the world through stunning photography captured by its audience. By encouraging users to share their travel photos featuring the hashtag #NatGeoTravel, National Geographic created a platform for photographers of all skill levels to showcase their work and connect with a global audience. The campaign generated millions of submissions and engagement from users around the world, solidifying National Geographic's reputation as a leading authority in travel and photography and driving brand awareness and engagement on Instagram.

These case studies of successful Instagram marketing campaigns demonstrate the power of the platform for engaging audiences, building communities, and driving business results. By leveraging compelling visuals, authentic storytelling, user-generated content, and strategic use of hashtags, brands can create impactful campaigns that resonate with their audience and drive engagement, brand awareness, and sales on Instagram. By studying these examples and applying the lessons learned to their marketing efforts, marketers can unlock new opportunities for success and achieve their business goals effectively on Instagram.

Conclusion:

In "Instagram Marketing for Business: A Step-by-Step Guide to Growing Your Audience and Building a Successful Brand on Instagram," we've explored the essential strategies, tactics, and best practices for leveraging the power of Instagram to achieve your business goals. From setting clear marketing goals and objectives to crafting compelling content, engaging with followers, and measuring success, this comprehensive guide has provided you with the tools and knowledge needed to succeed on the platform.

Throughout the book, we've emphasized the importance of authenticity, creativity, and audience engagement in driving results on Instagram. By building a strong brand identity, fostering meaningful connections with your audience, and delivering value through your content, you can create a loyal and engaged community of followers who are passionate about your brand.

We've also highlighted the significance of data-driven decision-making in optimizing your Instagram marketing strategy. By regularly analyzing performance metrics, monitoring trends, and adapting your approach based on insights, you can continuously improve your effectiveness on the platform and drive meaningful results for your business.

As you embark on your Instagram marketing journey, remember to stay agile, adaptable, and innovative in your approach. Experiment with new features, test different strategies and stay informed about industry trends to stay ahead of the curve and maintain a competitive edge on the platform.

Thank you for joining us on this journey through "Instagram Marketing for Business." Whether you're a small business owner, entrepreneur, marketer, or social media enthusiast, we hope this guide has equipped you with the knowledge and inspiration needed to thrive on Instagram and build a successful brand that resonates with your audience.

Now, it's time to put what you've learned into action and embark on your own Instagram marketing adventure. Here's to your success and growth on Instagram!

www.ingramcontent.com/pod-product-compliance
Lightning Source LLC
Chambersburg PA
CBHW082107220526
45472CB00009B/2086